BATTLE STATIONS

BATTLE STATIONS

Peter Gammons

KINGSWAY PUBLICATIONS
EASTBOURNE

Printed in Great Britain for
KINGSWAY PUBLICATIONS LTD
Lottbridge Drove, Eastbourne, E. Sussex BN23 6NT by
Richard Clay (The Chaucer Press) Ltd, Bungay, Suffolk.
Typeset by Nuprint Services Ltd, Harpenden, Herts.

Contents

TO
Ken and Joy Gammons, my parents,
whom I love dearly and for whom I am
so grateful to God

Acknowledgements

My thanks go to Maureen Ozenbrook, Rosemary Ellison and Anne Bird who have tirelessly typed and retyped this work.

Also to the Rev Danny Sneed, Michael Darwood, Alistair Forrest and Pat Darwood who have helped so much in the editing and preparation of this manuscript for print.

To the Rev Peter Harding, the Rev Don Double and the many others whom God has used in building into my own life the truths I have shared in this book.

Also to a dear saint of God, Miss Freda Woolstenholmes, whose life and faith in God have been a real example to me

Introduction

Christians often comment nostalgically to me, 'I wish I had been round during the days of the early church, Spurgeon, Wesley, or the Welsh Revivals, don't you?' And my answer is no. Although there have been many outstanding periods in the past, there is no other time when I would rather be alive than now. I believe that we are on the verge of a mighty move of God, unparalleled in church history, which Spurgeon, Wesley and many other of God's saints would have loved to experience.

Jesus impressed upon his disciples the privilege which was theirs of living in 'the last days', for 'many prophets and righteous men longed to see what you see but did not see it' (Mt 13:17 NIV). How much greater is our privilege, living in the latter part of the last days, literally the last of the last days (Acts 2:17). *You* have been chosen for this unique part in the climax of the ages. I believe this grand finale will be no anti-climax. What a joy to realize that *you* have come to the kingdom for 'such a time as this' (Esther 4:14).

People often talk of the church 'wrestling' against the powers of darkness, but they speak as if its losing so many rounds that the only hope is for Christ to return soon and remove us from the ring, before we are completely defeated. This is far from the picture the Scriptures give us. Christ is coming for a 'glorious church, not having spot or wrinkle or any such thing' (Eph 5:27). The church is a triumphant army moving into Satan's strongholds, and releasing his captives by the authority of their King, Jesus. Not 'Cluster's Last Stand'!

Although ultimate victory awaits Christ's return, that should be the climax of an ongoing victory in which we are involved right now. Every Christian is called to be an 'overcomer'. 'For whatever is born of God overcomes the world. And this is the victory that has overcome the world—our faith' (1 Jn 5:4). The ability to overcome is not something which we earn; we are born overcomers at our new birth. God intends victory to be the norm—and not only victory in our personal lives. We should be on the offensive, as well as the defensive, and win the victory as we invade the 'strong man's house and plunder his goods' (Mt 12:29).

A look through history reveals that times of insecurity, unease and a dissatisfaction with the religious life of the day have paved the way for revivals. God has promised that 'he will sift out everything without solid foundations, so that only unshakable things will be left. *Since we have a kingdom nothing can destroy*, let us please God by serving him with thankful hearts and with holy fear and awe. For our God is a consuming fire' (Heb 12:27–29 TLB). The things in the world in which people once put their trust, no longer provide security. You can hold a key job one day and lose it the next; be a national leader one day and deposed the next; be at the top of the entertainment world one day and finished the next. In our crumbling world there is only one place of true security: in the kingdom of God. God's kingdom is unshakable! The result of God's shaking in 'all the nations' is that they shall come to 'the Desire of All Nations' (Hag 2:7) and the glory of 'this latter temple' (Hag 2:9) shall be greater than the former!

A key word on the lips of God's people is *restoration*. *Cassells English Dictionary* defines the word 'restore' as 'to bring back to a former state, to repair, to reconstruct, to put back, to replace, to return; to bring back to health, to cure; to bring back to a former position, to reinstate…to renew…to represent as it is supposed to have been originally'. God's plan is to restore to us all that Adam lost through sin, with a plus: all the power of God that we read of in the book of Acts! We will see King Jesus restored to his rightful place as Lord of all.

How we need God to open our eyes to these truths. It is only he who can do it. Many Christians are doctrinally sound and yet there is little evidence that what they believe is real to them. If we are honest before God we have to admit that we know more than we live. True knowledge is much more than a head full of scriptural facts. I wonder how many messages we listen to without hearing what God is saying to us? God desires his people to live in reality. If we are going to have any effect on our world which is crying out for reality, it is imperative that the truths contained in this book become real in our lives. We must not hurry through it in one sitting, and then rush on to our next Christian book, but study it slowly, chapter by chapter, letting God speak to us his message for his people today.

The apostle Paul was not content to leave the Christians at Ephesus with heads full of facts, however biblical those facts might be, but prayed for them that 'The God of our Lord Jesus Christ, the Father of glory, may give to you the Spirit of wisdom and revelation in the knowledge of him, the eyes of your understanding being enlightened; that you may know what is the hope of his calling, what are the riches of the glory of his inheritance in the saints, and what is the exceeding greatness of his power towards us who believe' (Eph 1:17–19). That is my prayer for you as you read this book. It is my heart's desire that God will use it as a tool in raising up and mobilizing his army. I trust that as you read these pages your eyes will be opened to see the King in his glory. I pray that you will recognize your calling, realize your inheritance in him and commit yourself to being part of the army that God is raising up. In a moment we will consider what Jesus 'began' (Acts 1:1) to do. What he began, he plans to continue, through us, on an ever-widening scale.

May the scribe who pens the closing chapter of church history record 'This was their finest hour.'

1

Another King

Have you ever considered the amazing impact a few believers empowered by the Holy Spirit made upon the world? Despite limitations in transport, with no printed New Testament or literature, television, radios or tape recorders, the gospel spread in a few years throughout the then known world. One comment made by the unbelievers was that the followers of Christ had 'turned the world upside down.' Have you ever longed for that kind of effectiveness?

In recent years we have seen some mighty moves of God throughout the world. Nevertheless, this is but the tip of the iceberg of what God wants to do in the days ahead. I believe that we are on the verge of a mighty revival, unparalleled in the history of the church. When true revival breaks out, unbelievers won't have to read the Christian magazines to find out that it has taken place! The works of our God will be the talking point out on the streets. How I long to hear godless men saying in our towns and cities, 'Those who have turned the world upside down have come here too.'

However, if we are going to hear these words, we need to ask ourselves what this message was that they proclaimed. Read on in Acts chapter 17: 'These who have turned the world upside down, have come here too. Jason has harboured them, and these are all acting contrary to the decrees of

Caesar, saying, There is another King—Jesus' (Acts 17:6–7). How often do *we* hear the message proclaimed that *'There is another King'*?

Turning the world 'upside down' was of course man's view of what was happening. In fact, the theology was wrong. The world was not being turned upside down, but back up the right way, the way that God had intended it to be. The church was his tool in restoring what Adam had lost.

The gospel of the kingdom

For many Christians the kingdom of God applies to some utopia where they will go to on death; a futuristic thing. However, Jesus spoke of his kingly rule coming into this world now. He made such comments as 'The kingdom of God is among you', 'The kingdom of heaven is at hand (Mt 4:17), 'The kingdom of God is within you' (Lk 17:21). Right from the start 'Jesus went about all Galilee, teaching in their synagogues, preaching *the gospel of the kingdom*, and healing all kinds of sickness and all kinds of disease among the people' (Mt 4:23). His forerunner, John the Baptist, had proclaimed the message, 'Repent, for the kingdom of heaven is at hand' (Mt 3:2).

What was Jesus' first message? 'After John was put in prison, Jesus came to Galilee, preaching the gospel of the kingdom of God saying, "The time is fulfilled, and the kingdom of God is at hand. Repent, and believe in the gospel"' (Mk 1:14–15). Even before his birth the angel said to Mary, 'He will reign over the house of Jacob for ever, and of his kingdom there will be no end' (Lk 1:33). When Jesus sent his disciples out, he sent them to 'preach the kingdom of God' and to heal the sick' (Lk 9:1–2). During his last days on earth before his ascension, what was it that he spoke of with his disciples? 'The things pertaining to the kingdom of God' (Acts 1:3).

What was Paul's message? 'He went into the synagogue and spoke boldy for three months, reasoning and persuading concerning the things of the kingdom of God' (Acts 19:8).

Even under house arrest during the last few years of his life, Paul 'received all who came to him, preaching the kingdom of God and teaching the things which concern the Lord Jesus Christ' (Acts 28:30–31). What was Philip's message at Samaria about? 'The things concerning the kingdom of God and the name of Jesus Christ' (Acts 8:12).

From Matthew to Revelation, the gospel message is clearly seen as the gospel of the kingdom. There is no other gospel. Although references are made to the 'everlasting gospel' (Rev 14:6–7), the 'gospel of grace' (Acts 20:24) and the 'gospel of God' (Rom 1:1–5), this gospel is still the gospel of the kingdom. The kingdom of God and the kingdom of heaven are synonymous titles in Scripture. Heaven is the kingdom's throne room.

Up the right way

When Adam sinned and rebelled against God, everything began to go out of order and 'upside down'. Sickness, family tension, frustration, depression, fear, pain, heartache and loneliness—things which God never intended man to experience—all became common. However, the gospel of the kingdom, is that King Jesus has come to turn things back up the right way!

On earth Jesus demonstrated his rule over sickness by healing all who came to him, opening deaf ears and blind eyes, raising the dead, healing the paralytics, epileptics and lepers. He demonstrated his kingship over the powers of darkness by casting out demons and destroying Satan's kingdom wherever he went. Furthermore he demonstrated his dominion over the elements as he calmed a storm, filled nets with fish, walked on water, and multiplied a boy's lunch to feed the multitudes.

A day in the life of…

Constant demands were made on Jesus, at all hours of the day, to minister to those in need. He even missed meals (Mk

3:20–21) to carry on his work. At Peter's house, following a busy day of ministry, he found his disciple's mother-in-law sick with a fever, so 'he touched her hand and the fever left her' (Mt 8:14–15). Later that same evening they brought to him many that were demon possessed and 'he cast out the spirits with a word, and healed all who were sick' (Mt 8:16).

As soon as it was discovered that he was around, the crowds gathered (Mk 2:1–2). On one occasion a whole city came to his door! (Mk 1:33). Another time the crowds were so great that he had to get on to a boat to teach (Mk 3:8–10). Even when he slipped away to spend time in prayer, his disciples searched for him saying, 'Everybody is looking for you.' In Galilee people sought to stop him leaving, yet he said, 'Let us go into the next towns, that I may preach there also, because for this purpose I have come forth' (Mk 1:38).

Keep up the good work

Recognizing the vastness of the harvest fields, Jesus 'called his twelve disciples together and gave them power and authority over all demons, and to cure diseases. He sent them to preach the kingdom of God and to heal the sick' (Lk 9:1–2). They returned excited that the kingdom had been extended. The kingdom of God gained ground with every person who responded to the message. Every demon who received an eviction order, yielded territory for King Jesus. Wherever the sick were healed the kingdom came.

However, there was still much work to do, so next Jesus sent out the Seventy saying, 'The harvest truly is great, but the labourers are few, therefore ask the Lord of the harvest to send out labourers into his harvest.… He who hears you hears me, he who rejects you rejects me, and he who rejects me rejects him who sent me!' (Lk 10:2,16). When they entered a town Jesus exhorted them to heal the sick and say to them 'the kingdom of God has come near to you'.

Following his ascension and enthronement, the Lord poured out the Holy Spirit upon the waiting 120 to continue the work he had begun (Acts 2:1). The same Holy Spirit who empowered Jesus' life and ministry (Lk 4:18–19) now dwelt in them! The book of Acts is the account of Jesus' ministry continued through ordinary men and women.

Have you ever considered the strange ending to the book of Acts, with Paul under house arrest? The reason for this is that it has not ended! The book of Acts is unfinished and will be until Christ returns.

In his earthly body Jesus was limited to being in one place at a time, but by pouring out the Holy Spirit upon us, his followers, he can now be in every city and town throughout every nation of the earth, at the same time. We are 'the temple of the Holy Spirit' (1 Cor 6:19). In Israel's past, people had to go to the temple. Now, God sends his temple to them! As the Father sent Jesus, so he sends us! We are the 'body of Christ', his physical representatives (Eph 1:23 and 1 Cor 12:27).

Jesus promised, 'Most assuredly, I say to you, he who believes in me, the works that I do he will do also; and greater works than these he will do, because I go to my Father' (John 14:12). Do we really believe this scripture? Jesus who has all authority, has delegated his authority to us, to continue the work on his behalf. He has chosen to reveal himself and minister his healing power and deliverance through us. The gates of hell are no defence against the church of God (Mt 16:18). It is this gospel of the kingdom that will turn the world upside down. It is this gospel of the kingdom that we are sent to proclaim.

Whatever will be, will be?

While Jesus walked on earth, his kingship was openly seen. He went '*preaching* and *showing* the glad tidings of the kingdom of God' He didn't just preach the gospel, he showed it, too. He came with full authority to change every work of Satan. His philosophy was not the common one of 'whatever will be, will be'. Usually that is a lie of the devil, who is out to make us settle for less than God wants for us. Many adopt a fatalistic attitude concerning the future. 'I'll wait until I die to find out whether I go to heaven or hell,' they say, failing to realize that by their acceptance or rejection of Jesus here and now they themselves choose where they will spend eternity. When a person gets sick, the devil whispers, 'whatever will be, will be. It must be the Lord's will.' Yet, when the leper came to Jesus saying, 'If you are willing you can make me clean', the Lord corrected this man's theology: 'I am willing; be cleansed' (Mt 8:2–3). We need to see that Satan is out to destroy lives, but God is on the side of health!

When Jesus heard of John the Baptist's death, he went away to spend some time on his own. However, seeing the multitudes following him, he had compassion on them. He didn't just reveal his compassion by saying sympathetically, 'Well, never mind, whatever will be, will be. There are many far worse off, let's hope that you get better soon.' He came as King, with power to change their situations.

When a great storm broke out and the waves began to fill the boat, Jesus' disciples cried out in desperation 'Lord, save us! We are perishing' (Mt 8:23–26). What did the Lord do? Did he stand up and say, 'It looks as though we're going down, lads. It must be God's will, let's sing a chorus as we go down, "Que sera, sera, whatever will be, will be"'? No, he rebuked the winds and the sea and they were silent. He turned to his disciples and said, 'Why are you fearful, O you of little faith?' In other words, 'Why didn't you do that? What did you have to wake me for?' The gospel of the kingdom is the most practical message!

Mary in sorrow at her brother's death, came to Jesus saying, 'Lord if you had been here, my brother would not have died' (Jn 11:32). Could you imagine Jesus, the King of kings, standing outside the tomb saying to the mourners, 'Thank you for coming to this funeral in memory of our dear brother, let's stand and sing together hymn number 344— "Que sera, sera, whatever will be, will be"'? No, he was the King, and as King he had authority to change the situation. As he spoke those words, 'Lazarus, came forth', the dead man came out alive and well (Jn 11:43–44).

We move now to a hillside, where five thousand men, plus

women and children, have gathered to hear the word of God. The disciples came to Jesus and said, 'It's getting late, why don't you send the people away so that they can go and buy some food?' (Gammons' paraphrase version!) Can you imagine their reaction when Jesus turned to them and said, 'You give them something to eat'?

He was implying, 'Why do you keep coming to me. Soon I'm going to leave you to carry on the work—you give them something to eat.' Quite shocked at Jesus' answer, they replied, 'We have here only five loaves and two fish' (Mt 14:17–20). As Jesus spoke the words 'Bring them here to me', I can visualize them stepping back thinking, 'Let's see what he does now.' Could you imagine Jesus turning and saying, 'There's not enough here for this crowd, we'd better sing a closing hymn together and all go home; let's all stand and sing, "Que sera, sera whatever will be, will be"'? No, he sat the people down, took the fish and bread and, looking up to heaven, he blessed and broke them. Then he gave them to his disciples to feed the multitudes! Don't forget that at that time there were still only five small loaves and two small fish! Can you imagine the disciples' excitement as they distributed them? Even after everyone had eaten as much as they wanted, the crumbs left over filled twelve baskets! (One basket each!)

As Jesus landed at Gadara, two demoniacs ran towards him (Mt 8:28–34). Could you imagine the Lord saying, 'Sorry I can't help you poor people, but we'll sing a hymn to cheer you up.'? *No*, he is King. Jesus commanded the demons to go and both men were instantly set free (Mk 5:1–20).

Jesus is King!

Born to be King

Prophets foresaw and spoke of the coming King (Is 9:6; Zech 9:9; Ps 2:6). At his birth, the Magi arriving from their pilgrimage asked, 'Where is he who has been born King of the Jews?' (Mt 2:2). Herod, recognizing Jesus as a contender for his throne, sought to destroy him. Nathanael hailed him as 'King of Israel' (Jn 1:49) and James and John (through their mother) requested honoured positions of authority in his kingdom (Mt 20:21). The multitudes wanted to take him by force and make him King and they hailed him as King on his triumphant entry to Jerusalem. Following his arrest, the Chief Priests charged him with 'Perverting the nation... saying that he himself is Christ, a King' (Lk 23:2). Pilate bluntly asked Jesus in the Judgement Hall, 'Are you a King then?' To which Jesus freely answered, 'You say rightly that I am a King. For this cause I was born, and for this cause I have come into the world' (Jn 18:37). Pilate, apprehensive about crucifying Jesus, introduced him to the Jews saying, 'Behold your King...shall I crucify your King?' (Jn 19:14–15). The soldiers plaited a crown of thorns and dressed him up in a purple kingly robe saying, 'Hail, King of the Jews!' (see Jn 19:2–3). Even the conviction, written above the cross in Hebrew, Greek and Latin (the three major languages of the day) was 'Jesus of Nazareth, the King of the Jews' (Jn 19:19). His crime was simply being the divinely appointed King!

Born to die

Yet, right from the start of Jesus' ministry, John the Baptist identified him as 'The Lamb of God who takes away the sin of the world' (Jn 1:29) and Jesus was clear about his mission, that he was born to die (Mt 17:22–23); 20:18–19). Christ came to set us free from bondage and reconcile us to God, to 'destroy the works of the devil'. From the very start, Satan was aware of Jesus' motivation and sought to destroy him, first by putting in Herod's heart a desire to assassinate him (Mt 2:1–16) and later by prompting evil men to take him to the brow of a hill and throw him over (Lk 4:16–30). However, Jesus' time had not yet come, so they couldn't touch him: 'Passing through the midst of them he went his way.' He made it clear that no one could take his life from him (Jn 10:18). He was in total control.

Satan not only tried to destroy him physically, but also spiritually, seeking in the wilderness temptations to cause

God to sin (Lk 4:6; Mt 4:1–11). He offered 'the heir of all things' (Heb 1:2) the kingdom he had come to redeem, on the condition that Jesus would worship him (the devil's long sought desire). However, his plans failed miserably as Jesus' words rang out, 'You shall worship the Lord your God, and him only you shall serve' (Mt 4:10).

In a final bid Satan stirred up the religious and political leaders to have Jesus destroyed. Yet what Satan (not being omnipotent—1 Cor 2:7–8) had intended for evil and what looked to the world as the greatest of mistakes, led to his own downfall. What appeared on the surface to be a defeat for Jesus was, three days later, openly seen as the greatest victory of all, when he arose triumphant from the grave. There are parallels with the account of Haman in the book of Esther, who out of hatred for the Jews and Mordecai, sought to destroy them, even going as far as erecting a gallows to hang Mordecai on. However, his plans were discovered and the King 'hanged Haman on the gallows that he had prepared for Mordecai' (Esther 7:10). That which Satan had intended for evil, God intended for good, and the gallows the devil prepared for the Son of God, sealed his own total defeat.

At the time of his arrest, Jesus asked the approaching soldiers, 'Who are you seeking?' 'Jesus of Nazareth,' came the reply (Jn 8:4–7). The impact of Jesus' words has been lost by the translators who have added the word 'he' to the words 'I am'. In the Greek the word 'he' is not there. Jesus' reply was simply, 'I am' (the name by which God revealed himself in the Old Testament). As Jesus spoke these words, his divinity and kingship, which had been largely concealed during the years he had walked on earth, was for a split second revealed and the highly trained and armed soldiers could not stand on their feet, but 'fell to the ground'. Imagine the humiliation as those mighty soldiers picked themselves up and brushed themselves off. Slain by the words of Jesus' mouth! I'm convinced that as they marched him into Jerusalem, they were fully aware that he was coming because he chose to, not because he had to!

Mission accomplished

Jesus' words from the cross, 'It is finished' (Jn 19:30), were no cry of defeat. Not 'I've had it', but rather a mighty shout of victory, 'I've done it. It is completed. Mission accomplished.' Even at his death, it was evident to all that he was in total control. The centurion, who no doubt had witnessed numerous crucifixions, knew what a cruel and long death it was, normally lasting days before the victim died. Yet, after fulfilling his mission, Jesus simply spoke the words, 'Father into your hands I commend my Spirit' and died. The centurion, now convinced, said, 'Truly, this man was the Son of God' (Mk 15:39). Jesus was in full control, even over his death. Three days later, by rising from the dead, he openly demonstrated the victory he had won.

On the cross Jesus undid all that Adam had introduced through sin, all the pain, slavery and misery of the reign of sin and death. He ministered a mortal blow to Satan and his kingdom. He 'disarmed principalities and powers, he made a public spectacle of them, triumphing over them' (Col 2:15). After victory in battle, Roman generals would return through the streets, leading behind them the defeated king and his army. The whole of the town would gather to mock and jeer at the prisoners. Jesus has made such a public spectacle of the defeated army of the kingdom of darkness!

Some Christians talk as though good and evil were equal forces, or at best as if God were slightly stronger than Satan. However, Jesus said, 'All power is given to me' (see Mt 28:18), and he meant *all*. The Greek word used here for power is *exousia*, meaning 'the power of rule or government, the power of judicial decision.' It was the word Pontius Pilate used (Jn 19:10) when he said, 'I have power to crucify you, and power to release you.' It refers to the judicial authority of a magistrate: his word must be obeyed! On earth Jesus stood out as 'one with authority', but now ascended and seated on the throne, he has all authority. He is 'King of kings and Lord of lords' (Rev 17:14; Rev 19:16). The government is upon his shoulders.

Jesus is King of England

Whilst we recognize that one day Christ *will* rule eternally and unchallenged, we need to see that the primary New Testament teaching was not that Christ will reign, but that he does reign. The kingdom of God is not something futuristic to speculate about, but something present. 'We see Jesus... *crowned* with glory and honour' (Heb 2:9), not we *shall* see. He is on the throne now. All things are in subjection under his feet (see Heb 2:7–8) and there is *nothing* that is not put under him.

'The Lord sits as King for ever' (Ps 29:10). This is not the devil's world!

'*The earth is the Lord's* and all its fullness, the world and those who dwell therein' (Ps 24:1). Men rule only within the boundaries of God's will.

'God is the *King* of all the earth' (Ps 47:7).

'The Lord has established his throne in heaven and *his kingdom rules over all*' (Ps 103:19).

'The Kingdom is the Lord's, and *he rules* over the nations' (Ps 22:28).

He is reigning now, and we are called to proclaim among the nations: 'The Lord reigns' (Ps 96:10). The Scriptures do not just teach that one day Jesus will reign, but that 'He must reign till he has put all enemies under his feet' (1 Cor 15:25). What tremendous assurance we should receive from this knowledge that Jesus is on the throne even in these traumatic days through which we are passing. Nothing can happen without his permission!

The end

I recently saw a film during a flight overseas to the mission field. It was one of those films which holds you in suspense right up until the last minute. Everyone knew who ought to win, yet right up until the end the enemy seemed to be having all of the victories. Then, about three minutes before the end of the film, the whole thing changed and what had seemed like an apparent disaster, proved to be a great victory. In the midst of the film, the enemy's minor victories looked massive, but at the end they were revealed for what they were—total defeat. A couple of months later I was flying again, on a different plane to a different destination, when the same film was shown. This time as I viewed it my reaction was completely different. Although the same battles were being fought, I knew even before they started what would happen. While other people were looking fearful and concerned, I could sit back and relax, I knew who was going to win!

While the people of our world sit in fear of the future overshadowed with the threat of nuclear war, for the Christians there need be no fear: the end result is already revealed (Rev 20–21).

Jesus is King!

He has the power to end it all any time he wishes, and one day he will do so. However, in his mercy he has allowed time for men to receive his new life. Although, in God's purpose, Satan is still on the loose and man is free to rebel against the Lord, it will not be this way for ever. The result is already finalized and there is nothing Satan can do to change the results.

In a Law Court, judgement is passed before the sentence is carried out. Judgement has been passed on Satan; therefore, the sentence is inescapable!

Jesus Christ is Lord

At present we do not see everything subject to Jesus, but we do 'see Jesus' who was made a little lower than the angels, but is *now* crowned with glory and honour (Heb 2:8–9). One day his victory will be revealed for all eternity, as all those who have rejected him, along with the devil and his angels, are cast in the lake of fire and the effects of the fall totally and permanently reversed, 'Amen, come, Lord Jesus' (Rev 22:20).

Throughout Scripture, we see God continually bringing

things into subjection to himself. The whole of history is moving towards the climactic event, when everything is to be brought into obedience to King Jesus (1 Cor 15:25–28; Heb 2:14–15). He begins with those who are willing, by choice, to bow the knee to him. One day every knee shall bow and every tongue confess that Jesus Christ is Lord (see Phil 2:10). Those on earth who have rejected him will see him in his glory and have to bow the knee and admit that they were wrong. For them it will be too late to be saved. Everyone who has ever lived, rich or poor, every leader, every atheist and every religious leader will be included. There, amidst the masses, will kneel Karl Marx, Lenin, Darwin, Confucius, Mohammed, Krishna, Moon and Mussolini, all having to confess, '*Jesus Christ is Lord*'.

Until that day, the Lord has planned to use *you* to take territory for the kingdom of God, but first you must bow the knee to Jesus and let him be Lord in your life. Will you?

The accusation made against the early church was that they were acting 'contrary to the decrees of Caesar, saying there is another King—Jesus'. Caesar had ordained that he alone be called 'lord', the one with maximum authority, the one to whom everything belonged, 'the Boss'. Everyone was called upon to worship and burn incense to him. A soldier would greet a civilian in the street with the words, 'Caesar is Lord', and he had to reply (if he wanted to stay alive) 'The Lord is Caesar'. However, Christians knew full well Caesar was not Lord. Therefore, when the soldiers greeted them with the words 'Caesar is Lord', they had no option but to reply, 'No, Jesus is Lord.' This led to tremendous persecution and many were martyred for the gospel's sake. Following Jesus is costly. It is easy to say, 'I'd die for you, Jesus', but are we willing to live for him? One of the proofs of whether we would die for him, is whether we will live for him and let him be Lord now!

It seems fair to assume that your work on earth hasn't finished yet (otherwise God would have taken you home). I would suggest therefore that the Lord does not want you to die for him but he does want you to live for him right now!

2

The Divine Transfer

'I will do what I want'

This is a common attitude and the one which led to Satan's downfall. Once an anointed angel, high on the list of responsibility in God's service, he chose to oppose God: 'I will be as God.' Before this time no one challenged God's rule and the whole host of heaven gladly obeyed his will. Now God's rival, accompanied by other angels who sought to follow him in his attempted coup, was cast out of heaven. Thus began Satan's attempt at establishing a kingdom independent of God.

After God completed the creation, he made man both to serve him and enjoy his fellowship. Soon into the peace and tranquillity, in camouflage, entered Satan. His plan—to entice Adam to fall in the same way he had fallen, to act independently of God, to establish his own kingdom. He said in effect, 'You have your rights, why should you do what God wants; he knows that if you disobey him and eat the fruit of the tree of the Knowledge of Good and Evil, you'll be as God.' (See Gen 3:5–6.)

'You have your rights.' It sounded appealing, rebellion against God often does. However, it always reaps evil. Man was cast out of the garden and banished from God's presence. In submitting to Satan's will, he became a member of Satan's kingdom. Instead of being God's friend, he became Satan's

24

slave. From this time onwards a sinful nature was passed on perpetually. Sinning became a 'natural' way of life.

In the New Testament Satan is called 'The God of this age' (2 Cor 4:4 NIV), 'The prince of this world' (Jn 14:30 NIV), and John wrote 'The whole world lies under the sway of the wicked one' (1 Jn 5:19). We need to recognize who is behind the conflict, unrest and break-up of our world and society. Some ask, 'Why did God allow Satan to disobey him?' In answering that we need to ask why God has allowed *us* to disobey and yet survive. The answer is clear. God did not make us to be robots, but gave us a free will whereby we can chose to obey or disobey. We have the choice.

When man sinned, a wall of separation came between the holy God and sinful man. A wall far more impenetrable than any wall that separates the East from the West. In the Old Testament Tabernacle this separation was typified by a thick curtain which separated the Holy Place where the priests ministered from the Holy of Holies where God's glory and presence dwelt. It was a clear reminder to all that man had no direct access to God. Only once a year could the High Priest go beyond the curtain into the Holy of Holies to make sacrifice for man's sin. However, Jesus, the Lamb slain for the sin of the world, came to make access to God for man. He made it clear that 'No one comes to the Father except through Me' (Jn 14:6). Jesus is the only means of access to God (Heb 10:19–22). The Scriptures record that as Jesus died, the curtain separating the Holy Places from the Holy of Holies was torn in two 'from top to bottom' (Mt 27:51). A way into God's presence was opened for us. Notice how the Scriptures clearly emphasize that it was torn from 'top to bottom' and not bottom to top. The whole thing was instigated and carried out by God. It was not man's doing, but God's.

The kingdom of Satan

The statement 'Everyone is a child of God' is totally unscriptural. The Bible tells us we were born under 'the power of darkness' (Col 1:13). Jesus said, 'You are of your father the devil.' In an attempt to make sure that his captives are unaware of their captivity, Satan permits a certain amount of 'restricted' freedom. Most non-Christians would be horrified at the suggestion that they are under Satan's dominion. After all their theme song is, 'I did it my way'.

The kingdom of self

'I'm right.'
   'I'll do what I want.'
   'I want my own way.'
The desire for everything to revolve around 'me' is the result of the sinful nature with which I am born. I sin because I have a sinful nature. We were 'born in sin' and separated from God. 'The wicked are estranged from the womb, they go astray as soon as they are born, speaking lies' (Ps 58:3). It is not long before a new born baby expresses the nature within. As long as everything goes the way he desires, everything is fine. However, when his will is opposed, or his parents refuse to give him his own way, it is soon evident how strong a will that 'sweet innocent child' has. David the psalmist said, 'I was brought forth in iniquity' (Ps 51:5)

Sinning is not primarily something a child learns by imitation. The child who screams when he does not want to go to bed and has a temper tantrum when his desire is not met, did not learn this behaviour from his parents. The child who hides his sweets, pretending he has none, when it is suggested he offers another child one, did not learn this craftiness from his parents. It comes naturally. Sadly, many parents, through a fear of upsetting or losing favour with their child, or even through sheer exhaustion, give in to their child's will, allowing their child to have his own way. However, the end result is almost inevitably a spoilt, selfish child set for the rest of his life on a course to get his own way and do whatever he wishes, whatever the cost. In the badly spoilt child we may see the future delinquent, criminal and rebel. As I have said, Satan seems quite content to let captives have their own way, as long as they go in direct opposition to God's will for their lives. Even much social action and kind behaviour is motivated by pride and a selfish desire to receive respect, or to be admired.

The kingdom of darkness has been likened to a sinking ship. Satan knows that for him and his kingdom the future is hopeless. He knows that mankind can be saved, though he cannot, but he plans to take as many with him to hell as he can. To keep his captives in his kingdom, he lets them think they are having their own way, unaware that the ship is sinking. Imagine a holiday cruiser which has been struck and has received irreparable damage. The captain, knowing the situation to be hopeless but not wishing to alarm his doomed passengers, makes an announcement over the ship's intercom: 'Today all the drinks are free. You can drink as much as you wish. All those in second class cabins may move into the first class cabins at no extra cost. All meals today are on the house, eat as much as you can. In fact, you can do whatever you like, we don't mind.' Overcome by the generosity of their deceitful captain, the passengers dive headlong into the vast array of indulgences offered them saying, 'What a wonderful captain we have, we've never been treated so well before.'

Godless men and women are like children at a fun fair, sitting on the roundabout, as it goes round and round, turning the steering wheel of the toy car in which they sit and yelling to their parents, 'Look, Mummy, I'm driving.' In reality the car is continuing along a predetermined course entirely beyond the child's ability to change. The Bible says we are captive to the law of sin (Rom 7:23). Sin takes us captive like a prisoner of war, making us its 'servant' (Rom 6:17–19). Sin never fully satisfies. Not realizing this, we think satisfaction will come with a deeper involvement. Still unsatisfied, we seek more and more, only to find we are more and more entangled and captive to the habit. The person who begins smoking, saying, 'I'm in control. I can stop when I like', soon discovers he has lost control. The drug pusher is content with starting his customers on some mild drug, assured that they will soon be captive and back for more. Paul described this condition in Romans 7:19, 'The good that I will to do, I do not do: but the evil I will not to do, that I practise.' 'O wretched man that I am! Who will deliver me from this body of death?' (v24)

'He who sins is of the devil, for the devil has sinned from the beginning. For this purpose the Son of God was manifested, that he might destroy the works of the devil' (1 Jn 3:8). Jesus came to repossess the world. However, we can only come to him on his terms. People may comment, 'I don't need God's forgiveness, I'm sure I'm good enough.'

'I always try to help others.'

'I'm no worse than anyone else.'

These are confessions of pride and selfishness. Such an attitude takes multitudes to hell.

Yet even on transfer to the kingdom of God, many still wish to continue going their own selfish way. As we look at our actions and life-style in the light of Calvary, so much is revealed as being of the kingdom of self: self-confidence in the things we do; self-pity; grumbling and touchiness when things go wrong or don't go the way we wish they would; self-seeking and irritability; self-indulgence; a feeling of self-importance, which causes resentment if anyone contradicts our wishes or the things we say; self-consciousness which hinders many from obeying God by praising and worshipping him the way he tells us to in Scripture, saying, 'What will other people think?' Selfishness is sin and the only answer to sin is repentance and cleansing in the blood of Jesus.

Man's fall did not catch God off guard. As an 'all knowing' God, he already had a well planned and perfect recovery programme before Adam even sinned (Gen 3:15). Paul describes the result of God's rescue plan for mankind this way: 'He has delivered us from the power of darkness and translated us into the kingdom of the Son of his love, in whom we have redemption through his blood, the forgiveness of sins' (Col 1:13–14).

One of the words for 'redeem' in Greek is *exagorazo*; *agorazo* means to buy and *ex* denotes to buy out. It was a term used especially for purchasing a slave out of the slave market.

Jesus entered the slave market of the world to buy us back.

We have already considered how man became Satan's slave by an act of rebellion against God. The sin nature was passed from father to child for 'through one man sin entered the world' (Rom 5:12). Adam was responsible as head of the human race. Eve was deceived, but Adam deliberately sinned, with his eyes open. If Jesus had had an earthly father, he too would have inherited a sinful nature and been born as Satan's slave like the rest of mankind. However, although an authentic human being, Jesus was not a fallen son of Adam, so Satan had no claim on him. Therefore he came to the world a free man. Had Jesus sinned, he would have come under Satan's control. So from Bethlehem to Calvary a battle raged as Satan sought to cause the perfect Son of God to sin. However, when Jesus died without once failing in the smallest detail, he totally and eternally defeated Satan. The penalty for sin was fully paid. Satan's claim upon mankind was broken. Jesus came into the slave market of the world, the only free man, and said, 'I'll take the lot!'

A slave is the property of his master and cannot buy his own freedom. Only a free man can buy slaves. The price Jesus paid to redeem us, was his own life. As true God, he was worth more than the whole of mankind put together, and thus he was able to take the punishment for the whole of mankind. As true man, holy and sinless, he could truly represent mankind as its substitute. I have been bought by Jesus and I am no longer Satan's property! The authority Satan once had in my life has been broken. Neither am I my own property, to obey my own will and desires. I have been bought with a great price (1 Cor 6:20). I have been transferred to God's kingdom. God's kingdom on earth is made up of people who have made him their King.

Jesus described this transfer as being 'born again'. It is an instant transfer from the kingdom of darkness to the kingdom of God. One moment you are a citizen of Satan's kingdom, without Christ and without hope, destined for hell, the next you have been transferred by a divine miracle into the kingdom of God. Jesus said, 'Most assuredly, I say to you, unless one is born again, he cannot see the kingdom of God' (Jn 3:3). Let alone enter! Being 'born again' is not a parabolic way of describing the experience, but a literal fact! Becoming a Christian means that we die to the old rule in our life and are 'born again' into the kingdom of God with a new King, a new Father, a new family, a new destiny, a new nature and a new purpose for living. The enslavement, pain, misery, disharmony and reign of sin have been broken.

Although birth is just the beginning, it is vital. Imagine if you were to ask someone when their birthday was, and they replied, 'Oh, I never had a birthday. I just gradually arrived as I am.'

Although some people may not remember the day of their new birth, there must have been one. There may have been a 'gestation period', when they gradually became aware of the Lord and the message of Salvation, but the new birth itself was an *instant transfer*.

I'm perfect

The statement 'no one is perfect' is untrue. Although no one has achieved perfection by his own attempt, the Bible tells us, 'For by one offering he has perfected for ever those who are being sanctified' (Heb 10:14). Now I have been cleansed by Jesus, I stand perfect in God's sight. Positionally I am 'perfect', experientially I am 'being sanctified'.

A very good friend of mine was saved because someone once said to him over a cup of coffee, 'Did you know that as far as God is concerned, I'm perfect?' Although his initial reaction was one of shock and surprise, he started seeking to find out how he, too, could stand before God that way. Forgiveness is God's free gift, something we could never buy or earn. For 'If we confess our sins, he is faithful and just to forgive us our sins and to cleanse us from all unrighteousness' (1 Jn 1:9).

When God forgives our sin, in his sovereignty, he chooses to remember it no more. He declared, 'I will forgive their iniquity, and their sin I will remember no more' (Jer 31:34).

Micah 7:18, 19 tells us that God has cast our sins into the depths of the sea. He will never bring them up again. As Corrie ten Boom once said, he has put a sign up for us saying, 'No fishing'. It is so easy to fish our sins out again, even though we have sought and received forgiveness for them. But for those who are in Christ 'there is therefore *now* no condemnation' (Rom 8:1). I do not have to wait until I get to heaven. It is now that there is no condemnation. However, many Christians walk around full of guilt. Satan, the accuser of the brethren, brings up things of the past in an attempt to cause the Christian to live under condemnation. He knows that now we have been reconciled to God, we have been called to a ministry of reconciliation and so in any way he can he will try to stop us fulfilling our ministry.

Tactic 1

For his first tactic he comes as 'Satan'. In the Greek *Satanas* means 'adversary' or 'false accuser'. He is a liar and the Bible tells us there is no truth in him. However, often his arguments sound very convincing! Satan fires his temptation at you, then instantly comes along saying, 'Fancy you thinking that, and you call yourself a Christian.'

Tactic 2

His second tactic is as the 'devil'—in the Greek, *diabolos*, meaning the 'accuser' or 'slanderer'. This time when he comes his accusations are true. You have committed the sin. 'You've gone too far now, you don't think God will forgive you, do you?' he says. 'You don't deserve fellowship with God.' This keeps many Christians from quickly turning to the Lord for cleansing. They think they have to prove they are sorry (a subtle form of penance) and this sometimes lasts for days and weeks.

The Holy Spirit convicts us of sin for our own good, to lead us to repent, but Satan's accusations are to condemn us. He doesn't want us to repent. So many Christians live under condemnation. Failure leaves them wondering if God could ever use them again, or would ever want to. However, the

Lord is an expert at taking failures and turning them into successes.

Moses had been a murderer, and at one time had been filled with fear and unbelief (Ex 4:1–12). To save their own lives Abraham and his son Isaac both lied concerning the true identity of their wives, even letting other men take them. Jacob stole his brother's inheritance by deceiving his blind father. Yet Abraham is known as the friend of God, and we worship the God of Abraham, Isaac and Jacob. The great king, warrior and psalmist, David, committed adultery with Uriah's wife and then, to cover up his sin, sent the man to his death. Yet God called David 'a man after his own heart'. The disciples all failed and deserted the Lord, yet they went on to become leaders in proclaiming the gospel of the kingdom. This is not to excuse sin. Where there is no true repentance, discipline is necessary, but, when we are willing to repent, to turn away from sin, and walk in obedience, we can know God's forgiveness.

The accuser of the brethren, waits to throw at you all he can, to get you to give up (and he does his homework well!). However, before our accuser, we can declare God's verdict of 'autrefois convict'; you cannot punish a man twice for the same crime. The punishment for each and every sin was paid in full nearly two thousand years ago at the cross of Calvary. God is not unjust and so when we come before him in repentance, his verdict is 'not guilty'.

If God has declared us not guilty, Satan cannot take us to a higher court! There isn't one! 'Who shall bring a charge against God's elect? It is God who justifies' (Rom 8:33). 'There is therefore *now* no condemnation to those who are in Christ Jesus who do not walk according to the flesh, but according to the Spirit' (Rom 8.1).

There is none...

Not now...nor in eternity!

We can walk free, totally forgiven, with God's words ringing in our ears: 'Not guilty!'

Case closed...for ever!

3

Victory!

We have considered how, though we are sinners, Jesus' death paid the penalty we deserved for our sin. But are we doomed to continual sin for the rest of our Christian life? 'Certainly not' (Rom 6:2). At the cross Jesus won a total victory. His death does not just deal with the penalty for our sin, but also with the power that drove us to sin. Not only can I enjoy fellowship with God for eternity, but here and now I can live in victory.

Satan, who is a 'liar' (Jn 8:44) and the 'deceiver of the brethren' wants us to believe the lie 'we are all sinners, while we are here on earth we always have to continually sin.' The main propagators of this teaching are 'Christian' ministers. They quote the apostle Paul as saying, 'For the good that I will to do, I do not do; but the evil I will not to do, that I practise...O wretched man that I am! Who will deliver me from this body of death?' (Rom 7:19, 24) to support their teaching and leave it there. Paul, however, does not leave it there, but goes on to answer his question: 'I thank God through Jesus Christ our Lord!' (v 25). There is victory in Jesus! Satan, recognizing that he cannot alter the fact of Christ's total victory, will do all that he can to stop Christians realizing and believing this truth. He knows that he cannot defeat Jesus, so his only chance now is to defeat you.

When I first became a Christian, I was told, 'You are a sinner, you'll always sin.' So I gave in, resigning myself to the fact that while I was here on earth I would never experience true victory. However, this is far from what the Bible teaches. Firstly in the Scriptures Christians are not referred to as sinners. Paul even called the carnal Christians at Corinth, 'Saints' (1 Cor 1:2)! I *was* a sinner, destined for hell, but by the grace of God he has saved me and made me a *saint*. Saints are not outstandingly gifted persons of bygone days, but people all of us are called to be.

Let there be light

The story is told of a mother who asked her little child during a church service what a saint was. The boy looked up at the stained glass windows around him which depicted the saints of days gone by and replied, 'A saint is someone who the light shines through.'

Every Christian is called to be a saint, one whom the light shines through! You were a sinner, but now in Christ you are no longer a sinner, but a saint, with the potential to live in victory, with the light of Jesus shining through. Holiness and victory are not things which God intends for the 'old few' to achieve, but are his standard for every saint. God rules in his kingdom with a sceptre of righteousness (Heb 1:8). It was a break-through in my life to discover that our lives do not have to be a vicious circle of sinning, repenting, sinning, repenting, but that we can have victory over the things that once had victory over us. I am not teaching that now we are Christians we will never sin again, but that we can live in victory. Paul did not claim to be perfect, but he did say, 'I press towards the goal' (Phil 3:14). 'I am on the way.' He had a goal. The holiness which is ours positionally needs to become evident experientially, evident in everyday life. It is wonderful to realize that '*we* are more than conquerors through him who loved us' (Rom 8:37) and that he '*always* leads us in triumph' (2 Cor 2:14). He 'is able to keep *you* from stumbling and to present *you* faultless before the presence of his glory with exceeding joy' (Jude 24). He is 'able to' keep *you*, if you will be kept. The potential is there. Many people talk about this verse as if it referred to heaven. When we are in heaven we will not need to be kept, nor will we ever fall again, it is *now* in this life that he is able to keep us from falling and to present us faultless!

Many Christians stop at 'Christ died for me'. It is a wonderful truth that we are forgiven and can face God fearlessly. However, in the New Testament it is equally expounded, yet missed by many today, that I died 'in Christ'. I died with him. Our sins can be forgiven, but our sinful nature cannot be forgiven, it must die. In Christ I am forgiven and a new creature. 'The old has passed away.' A realization of the truth that 'I have died with Christ', is vital to living in victory. This is not something which is going to happen, but a past *historical fact*. That I have died, is as much a fact as that Christ died for me (Rom 6:4). By faith we see that not only did Jesus die for us, but that we went to the cross with him. Paul puts it this way—'knowing this, that our old man *was* crucified with him, that the body of sin might be done away with, that we should no longer be slaves of sin. For he who has died *has been* freed from sin' (Rom 6:6). It is interesting to note how many times Paul uses such words as 'knowing this' or 'we know'. A true knowledge of this teaching makes all the difference. We need to reckon ourselves dead; and dead people don't sin!

Dead!

The story is told of two girls who, after becoming Christians, felt that it would be wrong for them to attend a wild party they had been invited to the next day. So they wrote a letter to the person who had invited them saying, 'Mary and Jane Brown regret that they will be unable to come to the party tomorrow because they died today.'

We are new creatures, the old has passed away. 'I have been crucified with Christ; it is no longer I who live, but Christ lives in me; and the life which I now live in the flesh I live by faith in the Son of God, who loved me and gave himself for me' (Gal 2:20). Not only have I died to the old rule of sin, but Jesus has come to live within me, to *live his life through me*. God does not call us to do something which he will not equip us to do. When Peter writes in 1 Peter 1:13–16: 'As he who called you is holy, you also be holy in *all* your conduct, because it is written, "Be Holy, for I am Holy"', we can actually do it. God does not dangle the carrot only to snatch it away when we go for it. When he says, 'Awake to righteousness and do not sin' (1 Cor 15:34) he means it.

'For *you died*, and your life is hidden with Christ in God' (Col 3:3). '*You died* with Christ' (Col 2:20). We died (past tense) and are now able to live for God's glory.

We are also able to live to please ourselves if we wish, the choice is our own. The cross deals with our old sinful nature, but not with our will. Sin is no longer your master, but it is up to you to 'not let sin reign in your mortal body, that you should obey it in its lusts and do not present your members as instruments of unrighteousness to sin, but present yourselves to God as being alive from the dead, and your members as instruments of righteousness to God. For sin shall not have dominion over you, for you are not under law, but under grace' (Rom 6:12–14). *The Christian sins by choice*. We still have a free will and can choose to sin if we want to. While we are here on earth the possibility to sin is always there. Temptation will still come.

An invitation to sin

Temptation is not sin; merely an invitation to sin, and we can reject the invitation. I anticipate accusations of preaching sinless perfection. This is not true. I know that I am not perfect and I am aware that there are still areas in my life which I do not yet realize God wants to deal with. However, I do believe we can have victory over the areas of sin we *are* conscious of! For 'to him who knows to do good and does not do it, to him it is sin' (Jas 4:17).

He has promised that 'Sin shall *not* have dominion over

you' (Rom 6:14). Jesus was tempted in all things as we are yet he did not yield to that temptation (Heb 4:15). Although he was truly God, he became man and lived in total victory, to demonstrate to us that such victory is possible for redeemed man. Jesus could have sinned, otherwise the temptations would not have been real, however he chose to obey God. Augustine put it this way, 'You can't stop the birds flying over your head, but you can stop them nesting in your hair.' It is not God who tempts us (Jas 1:13). However, he allows us to be tempted—not for defeat but for victory. The answer to defeat is not immunity to temptation, but to live in the victory which Jesus won for us.

Being a Christian does not mean we will never sin. We still can, but we do not have to and if we desire to please God we will not want to. There is no longer any compulsion to sin (1 Jn 2:1, 2). In his first Epistle, John makes it clear that the purpose of his writing is 'so that you may not sin'. Then he goes on to say, '*If* anyone sins, we have an advocate with the Father, Jesus Christ the righteous. And he himself is the propitiation for our sins, and not for ours only but also for the whole world.' Note, the Scriptures say, *if* any man sins, not *when*. God does not take it as a foregone conclusion that we will sin!

Red carpet living

The truth of this came alive to me one free weekend when, after a busy itinerary, a Christian businessman I knew contacted me to say, 'I've arranged to take you away for a break to a little hotel I know.' As he drove down to London I questioned him (unsuccessfully) about our destination. Then he suddenly made a sharp right hand turn revealing in front of me in big bold letters the word SAVOY. With my cases carried to my rooms, jacket brushed, car washed and polished, whilst I relaxed in a spa bath, I felt like a king. I really enjoyed walking up and down the thick red carpet steps to my room. At my window there was a fire escape, in case it was needed. However, I never used it once. I was living in 'red carpet area'. Through Jesus' death on the cross we can live in victory over temptation. The fire escape is provided, if we need it. '*If* anyone sins, we have an advocate with the Father' (1 Jn 2:1), but God never intended us to spend the rest of our Christian life up and down the fire escape, but in red carpet area.

That is why James could write, 'My brethren, count it all joy when you fall into various trials (or temptations), knowing that the testing of your faith produces patience. But let patience have its perfect work, that you may be perfect and complete, lacking nothing' (Jas 1:2–4). If it were impossible to live in the victory, to suggest that we could be joyful when we are tried would be ridiculous. I remember well, early in my Christian life, being confused when I first read these verses. This was not the picture I had been given concerning temptation. My attitude had been one of despair: 'Oh no, not another temptation, I'll only fall.' Certainly I felt no joy! I decided I would look up this verse in other translations to see what they said, to see if this was a misprint in my Bible. However, other translations said such things as 'count yourself fortunate', 'be happy'. Why? Because we can live in victory. Our reaction can be positive: 'Lord, I know in my own strength I would fail, but in you I can be more than a conqueror and by resisting this temptation it is another opportunity for me to grow stronger' (see Rom 8:37).

As I resisted in areas that were once major battle zones and said no to the temptations, they ceased to be the same problem. The Bible is clear, 'No temptation has overtaken you, except such as is common to man, but God is faithful, who will not allow you to be tempted beyond what you are able, but with the temptation, will also make the way of escape that you may be able to bear it' (1 Cor 10:13). Isn't it tremendous to realize that whatever temptation God allows, we will be able to have victory over it!

'The devil made me do it' is no excuse. Equally invalid are the old excuses, 'You don't know what it is like for me you've never had it as hard as I do' or 'I could never live in victory with that person around'. The Bible is clear, '*no* temptation has overtaken you except such as is *common* to man.' Although the temptation that you are experiencing at this time may be different to the one someone else is experiencing, it is no harder, and you can have victory as much as they can.

This truth is illustrated by the story of the little lad who was shopping with his mother. Another shopper watched as the boy carried the basket while his mother took the goods from the shelf and placed them into it. The observer was getting increasingly concerned as more and more articles were added until she could hold back no longer and stormed up to the young lad saying, 'Isn't that mean of your mother putting those heavy things into your basket and making you carry it.' The little lad innocently replied, 'Oh no, my mother knows just how much I can carry and will not put in more than I can bear.' That is true of our Heavenly Father, he will not allow you to be tempted above where you are able to stand in victory. Sometimes when God increases the pressure it may seem 'too heavy', but it's not. *It just shows you are growing!*

There are certain principles which I believe are important for victorious living.

(a) *You must be born again*

The victory I have been talking of is not possible unless you have become a 'new creature'. We have already seen that from birth a child is born with a sinful nature and that we do not have to teach our children to sin. However, we have also seen that Jesus came to set us free and when he died on the cross he took to that cross the old sinful nature which had driven us to sin so that we might live in victory. 'What shall we say then? Shall we continue in sin that grace may abound? Certainly not! How shall we who died to sin live any longer in it?' (Rom 6:1–2).

'...Reckon yourselves to be dead indeed to sin, but alive to God in Christ Jesus our Lord' (v 11).

'...having been set free from sin, you became slaves of righteousness' (v 18).

'...Now having been set free from sin, and having become

slaves of God, you have your fruit to holiness, and the end, everlasting life. For the wages of sin is death, but the gift of God is eternal life in Christ Jesus our Lord' (v 22–23).

It is in Christ that we are new creatures, dead to sin, alive to God, free to choose whether to sin or obey God, with the potential to be those he always causes to triumph!

(b) *Know how Satan attacks*

Understanding your enemy's tactics is a fundamental requirement for success in a military campaign. Satan's tactics, however, are not very original and the battle ground is the mind. Evil actions begin as evil thoughts, as a man 'thinks in his heart, so is he' (Prov 23:7). Mental discipline is vital to victory as Satan never takes a holiday. David recognized where the battle was and said, 'How long must I wrestle with my thoughts' (Ps 13:2 NIV). Satan's question to Eve, 'Did God really say, "You must not eat from any tree in the garden?" … You will not surely die' (Gen 3:4 NIV), was an attack on her thought life. Eve ate of the fruit in her mind before she physically ate of it. David committed mental adultery before he committed physical adultery. Satan's attack on Jesus was a mental attack, 'If you are the Son of God'. He sought to put doubt in Jesus' mind as to his true identity: 'If you are who you say you are and who God has just said you are, prove it by doing this, this and this.' His temptations always sound so reasonable!

I remember once being told by a sports coach, 'You give up first in your mind, then your body quits.' We need to see that whatever controls a man's thoughts, controls the man. 'The weapons of our warfare are not carnal, but mighty in God for pulling down strongholds, casting down arguments and every high thing which exalts itself against the knowledge of God, bringing every thought into captivity to the obedience of Christ' (2 Cor 10:4–5). It is our responsibility to bring every thought into captivity, to give the enemy no place (Eph 4:27). Refuse entrance to those negative, critical, resentful, impure, unkind, evil, unjust or envious thoughts. Satan as a roaring lion is seeking those whom he may devour

(1 Pet 5:8). This should alert us to be 'sober and vigilant'. Those were words used of a soldier on guard duty. It was his responsibility to be on the alert, recognizing that the enemy might attack at any time. Guard zealously your thought life: 'Whatever things are true, whatever things are noble, whatever things are just, whatever things are pure, whatever things are lovely, whatever things are of good report, if there is any virtue and if there is anything praiseworthy meditate on these things' (Phil 4:8). This is a good test for anything we intend listening to, saying, watching or reading. It would make a good text to put on top of television sets with an added note, 'If a programme does not come into these categories there is an Off switch provided!' What goes into a person will decide what comes out.

It is true also that we get like the people we spend our time with. 'Do not be deceived; evil company corrupts good habits' (1 Cor 15:33). If you find the wrong things are coming out in your life, take a look at what is going in. The Bible is clear, 'Whatever a man sows that he will also reap' (Gal 6:7). If you allow all kinds of junk to go into your life it is inevitable that junk will come out. The man who sows weeds in his garden can blame no one but himself for the resultant crop of weeds.

(c) *You must want to live in victory*

This may sound a strange or obvious thing to say. However I believe that it is the major key. It is our responsibility to 'Flee also youthful lusts; but pursue righteousness, faith, love, peace with those who call on the Lord out of a pure heart' (2 Tim 2:22). As we have already seen, there are things which we are to run from (flee) and others we need to run after (pursue). Yet many Christians are running in the wrong direction!

A good example of this fleeing can be found when Potiphar's wife enticed Joseph to her room seeking to get him to commit adultery with her. The Bible makes it clear he did not just sit back saying, 'As a servant of God I don't believe in that kind of thing, but I'll have a cup of tea with you and explain why.' He ran from the room. He fled from sin (Gen

39:11–12). Many a Christian has committed sin because they thought they were strong enough to stay around when tempted. Let us be on our guard 'therefore let him who thinks he stands take heed lest he fall' (1 Cor 10:12).

The choice is our own. God will keep us if we will be kept. It is our responsibility to refuse temptation (Tit 2:11–12). It is our responsibility not to let sin reign. 'Do you not know that to whom you present yourselves as slaves to obey, you are slaves of the one whom you obey, whether of sin to death, or of obedience to righteousness' (Rom 6:16).

'Therefore *do not let* sin reign in your mortal body, that you should obey it in its lusts, and *do not present* your members as instruments of unrighteousness to sin, but present yourselves to God as being alive from the dead, and your members as instruments of righteousness to God' (Rom 6:12–13).

In the past we chose to use our minds and bodies sinfully, now we are called upon to yield our minds, wills and bodies to the Lord. 'Lord, I give you my hands, I give you my eyes, I give you my affections, I surrender my will to your will, I surrender the right to choose how they are used, they are mine no more, but now they are yours. I yield them to you.'

'Therefore submit to God. Resist the devil and he will flee from you' (Jas 4:7). It is only as we submit ourselves to God and his will that our resisting of the devil is effective. Until Satan is convinced that I will obey God in an area of my life, that area will be under constant attack.

(d) *Get buried*

Now that you have died, you need to be buried. Of all the areas of victorious Christian living this is one that has been watered down (excuse the pun) more than any. For many, baptism is regarded as an 'optional extra' for those who want it. For others it is regarded as a nice ceremony to bless the saints, or a good excuse to invite the unsaved in. For some it is an 'outward sign of an inward grace'. Many regard it as an important step of obedience. For others it is used as a reward. If the person has completed a teaching series or stood as a Christian for so many months then they may be baptized.

However, I do not believe any of these are the primary purpose for baptism in Scripture. Water baptism for believers was taught as a basic part of the gospel message. In reply to the crowd's questions to Peter and the rest of the apostles, 'Men and brethren, what shall we do?' Peter said, '*Repent*, and let every one of you *be baptized* in the name of Jesus Christ for the remission of sins; and you shall *receive the gift of the Holy Spirit*' (Acts 2:37–38). It was not an optional extra, but rather something which the apostle Paul *commanded* Cornelius' household to do following their conversion (Acts 10:48). Nor was it a reward for good behaviour, but something which immediately followed a person's conversion, even, as in the Philippian jailor's experience, at midnight: on believing 'immediately he and all his family were baptized' (Acts 16:33). The New Testament norm was not even to wait for the next public service!

Jesus' command was, 'Go therefore and make disciples of all nations, baptizing them in the name of the Father, and of the Son and of the Holy Spirit, teaching them to observe all that I have commanded you' (Mt 28:19). It was not, 'Go therefore and make disciples of all the nations teaching them to observe all that I have commanded you and then baptizing them.' In the New Testament there was no waiting period between becoming a Christian and being baptized. Nor was it primarily a 'testimony to the world'. There is no implication that any unsaved were present at the Philippian jailor's baptism or when the Ethiopian eunuch believed. 'Now as they went down the road, they came to some water. And the eunuch said, "See, here is water. What hinders me from being baptized?" Then Philip said, "If you believe with all your heart, you may," and he answered and said, "I believe that Jesus Christ is the Son of God." So he commanded the chariot to stand still. And both Philip and the eunuch went down into the water, and he baptized him' (Acts 8:36–38).

Neither is baptism just an outward sign of an inward grace! Rather it is a burying of the old man that died in Christ. 'Therefore we were buried with him through baptism into death, that just as Christ was raised from the dead by the glory of the Father, even so we also should walk in newness of life. For if we have been united together in the likeness of his death, certainly we also shall be in the likeness of his resurrection' (Rom 6:4–5). The Scriptures do not say baptism is a type of being buried with him but, 'We were buried with him through baptism.' I see by faith, that as I go down under the water, in Christ I died to my old life and lifestyle and am now buried and arise out of the water to a new life, a life of victory. 'Buried with him in baptism, in which you also were raised with him through faith in the working of God, who raised him from the dead' (Col 2:12).

It is as I realize this truth that I can move in by faith and live in the reality of it. It was not until we realized Christ took our sin to the cross that we could move in and enjoy the benefit of his death for us. The same is true when I realize that I was buried with him by baptism. That is why Satan will try to stop saints understanding the importance of baptism for their walk with God.

(e) *Be baptized in the Holy Spirit*

The baptism in the Holy Spirit is not an optional extra either, but a vital necessity for living the life to which God has called us. We need to realize that he is the *Holy* Spirit and one of his major purposes is to make us a holy people. John the Baptist referred to Jesus as the one who would 'baptize you with the Holy Spirit and fire' (Mt 3:11).

One of our major uses for fire is to burn up rubbish. In the same way, one of the major purposes of the baptism in the Holy Spirit is to burn up the rubbish in our lives. We call it sanctification. It is he who will lead you into all truth. It is he who convicts the world of sin, righteousness and judgement. The life where the Holy Spirit is in control will be a life of holiness. We will consider this subject further in the next chapter.

(f) *Stand with one another*

How we need other Christians! Have you noticed in the verse we looked at earlier that we are to 'Flee also youthful lusts;

but pursue righteousness, faith, love, peace *with those* who call on the Lord out of a pure heart' (2 Tim 2:22). Our walking in victory is 'with those' who call on the Lord. We need one another to encourage us, confront us and provoke us to walk with the Lord.

There will be times when we need to share with those close to us areas in our lives where we are having battles so that they might pray with us and stand with us in those battles. How we need to be real. God did not intend us to go through life all alone. We need those to whom we can confess our faults (Jas 5:16).

We can never justifiably condemn one another. We have already seen that no one is immune to temptation and that 'No temptation has overtaken you except such as is common to man' (1 Cor 10:13).

The Scriptures give a clear warning to those who would seek to condemn another Christian: 'Let him who thinks he stands, take heed lest he fall' (1 Cor 10:12). We need one another. This is especially true of those in leadership. They are under strong attack for Satan is aware that if he can succeed in striking the shepherd, the sheep will be scattered. Yet so often, through fear of what others will think or fear of damaging their reputation, they go it alone, with no one to stand with them. This has led to the downfall of many a leader. We need those with whom we can build strong relationships of trust and to whom we can open our heart in confidence, so that we can live in the victory which is ours through Jesus.

I am aware that there is so much more that could be said on this subject, yet I trust that what I have shared will help you to live in the victory which is yours in Christ.

4

Dynamite

Although Jesus was conceived by the Holy Spirit, his public ministry did not begin until he had been empowered by the Holy Spirit. This occurred on the occasion of his baptism by John in the River Jordan. From then onwards the supernatural became natural. Wherever he went, demons cried out, captives were set free, peoples' needs were met and the sick were healed. No doubt from birth Jesus would have regularly attended the synagogue. Yet now when he entered, those possessed by demons began to scream out. What was different? Jesus attributed these things to the empowering of the Holy Spirit. He said, to the people in the synagogue: 'The Spirit of the Lord is upon me, because he has anointed me to preach the gospel to the poor. He has sent me to heal the broken-hearted, to preach deliverance to the captives and recovery of sight to the blind, to set at liberty those who are oppressed, to preach the acceptable year of the Lord' (Lk 4:18–19).

During his earthly ministry Jesus was limited to being in one place at one time. On a number of occasions prior to his death he told his disciples that he intended to leave them (Mt 3:16, Mk 1:10–11). However, the penny had not dropped—they were either unable or unwilling to receive this information, having learnt from bitter experience that they were weak without Jesus around. What an apparently hopeless bunch they were. At his arrest they all denied and deserted him. Peter even denied him to a servant girl. Thomas refused to believe that Jesus had risen unless he had physical evidence and as they gathered in the upstairs room after the resurrection the remembrance of Judas' betrayal of Jesus and suicide was fresh in their minds.

How could such a group make any impact on their world? Jesus was far more aware of their weakness than they were. Therefore, he had told them: 'Tarry in the city of Jerusalem until you are endued with power from on high' (Lk 24:49). He had commanded them not to leave Jerusalem, but to wait for 'the promise', explaining that they would be baptized in the Holy Spirit, and empowered for the work to which he had called them. Jesus compared this empowering to John's baptism. As John had immersed those who came to him in the River Jordan, so Jesus would totally immerse them in the Holy Spirit. He went on to explain, 'You shall receive power when the Holy Spirit has come upon you and you shall be witnesses to me in Jerusalem, and in all Judea and Samaria, and to the end of the earth' (Acts 1:8). I'm convinced that they realized that such an empowering must be something amazing if it was going to turn them into 'witnesses' for him throughout the earth! I can well imagine the thought going through their minds as Jesus unveiled his mission for them.

'Jerusalem'

'Oh no, not Jerusalem, we denied you here a few days ago, Jesus! Can't you send us somewhere else, where we're unknown, to start again?' (I've noticed that before the Lord calls us to some remote country to be witnesses, he first sends us back to our locality, to our own homes and families and employment to be witnesses for him. Yet so many Christians want to run.)

'And Judea'

'That's rather a large area to cover, Jesus, can't you send us to some smaller place? You're expecting too much of us.'

'And Samaria'

'You know we're good Jews, Jesus, we have nothing to do

with the Samaritans.'
'*And to the ends of the earth*'
'Let's go home!'

This baptism in the Holy Spirit must be a powerful experience. Jesus had said they would receive 'power' when the Holy Spirit came upon them. This word comes from the Greek word *dunamis*—from which we get our English words, dynamite, dynamic and dynamo.

As Jesus promised, when the day of Pentecost had come, while they were all with 'one accord' in one place, suddenly there came a sound from heaven, a sound as of a rushing mighty wind, which filled the whole house where they were sitting. Then there appeared to them forked tongues, as of fire, and one sat upon each of them. And they were 'all filled with the Holy Spirit and began to speak with other tongues, as the Spirit gave them utterance' (Acts 2:1–4). The baptism in the Spirit was to revolutionize their lives. The dynamic effect was evident to all. It drove this timid fearful bunch out into the streets of crowded Jerusalem. Peter now empowered by the Spirit, stood up and began to preach, and three thousand were converted! This was the same Peter who days before had denied the Lord rather than reveal his identity as a follower of Christ. I have heard it taught by those who cannot understand the dynamic change in Peter that this was a different man to the Peter in the gospels!

If you had asked Peter, 'Have you received the baptism in the Holy Spirit yet?' I'm convinced he wouldn't have said, 'I don't know.' When you have, you know it. The baptism in the Spirit is not an optional extra, nor is it just a theory or doctrinal opinion, but a necessary empowering for every Christian to live the life to which God has called us; a *vital* precondition to an effective Christian walk. The word for 'power' (*dunamis*) can also be translated 'ability'. The power of the Holy Spirit came to transform even the inexperienced and mostly uneducated disciples into useful witnesses for him. It brings the ability to do all that God calls us to do. If Jesus himself needed to be empowered by the Holy Spirit how much more do we?

To go out into the world without being empowered by the Holy Spirit is like going to war with blanks in our weapons! We can work our fingers to the bone to no effect. Attempts at evangelism without the empowering of the Holy Spirit is like trying to drive a car without an engine. 'For though we walk in the flesh, we do not war according to the flesh. For the weapons of our warfare are not carnal but mighty in God for pulling down strongholds, casting down arguments and every high thing that exalts itself against the knowledge of God, bringing every thought into captivity to the obedience of Christ' (2 Cor 10:3–5). *Dynamite*! Put dynamite under somebody's chair and you see a difference!

Greater things

In John 14 Jesus said that we his followers would do greater things than he did, because he was going to the Father. After his return to the Father and his crowning as Lord of all, he poured out the Holy Spirit upon us so now each one of us can continue the things which he began. The book of Acts starts by referring to the things which Jesus began to do. These have never ceased. What Jesus began to do in the limitations of his physical body, he now plans to continue throughout the whole world through his church, the body of Christ on earth. Now he is not limited to being in one place at one time. At the same time as he is in Jerusalem he can be in Capernaum, New York, London, Paris, Tanzania and in every country and city in the world.

The same Holy Spirit who empowered Jesus indwells the believers. To say, 'But that was Jesus' is no excuse. He wants to do greater things through you! (Jn 14:12–18). Jesus said that the Holy Spirit would flow through the believer: 'Out of your innermost being shall flow rivers of living water.' Anyone who gets near—gets wet!

Let us not confuse the baptism in the Holy Spirit with either the new birth or baptism in water. Although each is distinct in Scripture they are closely connected as foundational parts of our Christian life. It seems that the norm in the early church was for people to be baptized in water as soon as they were saved. At the same time they had hands laid on them to receive the baptism in the Spirit (Acts 2:38). 'Repent, and let every one of you be baptized in the name of Jesus Christ for the remission of sins, and you shall receive the gift of the Holy Spirit.' On many occasions I have known people to be baptized in the Holy Spirit within minutes of being saved (and some baptized in water, too). Salvation is God's free gift to the sinner. The baptism in the Holy Spirit is God's free gift to the saints.

In Acts 8 we read of how, due to great persecution, the believers were being scattered and of Philip going down to Samaria, where he 'preached Christ' to them (v 5). Tremendous miracles and deliverances followed the preaching of the word and the people 'with one accord heeded the things spoken by Philip' (v 6). They believed and were baptized (v 12). The city was filled with 'great joy' (v 8). However, when the apostles in Jerusalem heard that Samaria had 'received the word' they sent Peter and John, who came down and prayed for them that they might 'receive the Holy Spirit' (8:14–17). 'For as yet he had fallen upon none of them. They had only been baptized in the name of the Lord Jesus. Then they laid hands on them, and they received the Holy Spirit.' There is no doubt that they were true believers before the apostles came down and laid hands on them to receive the Holy Spirit. Philip's encounter with the Ethiopian eunuch makes it clear that he would not baptize anyone unless they 'believed with all their heart that Jesus Christ is the son of God' (8:36–37).

Paul too was converted on the Damascus road, but later healed, filled with the Holy Spirit and afterwards baptized in water (9.1–17).

At Ephesus (Acts 19) the believers were visited and asked the question, 'Did you receive the Holy Spirit when you believed?' To which they replied that they had not heard of the Holy Spirit and had only been baptized by John. After being baptized in water, hands were then laid on and, 'The Holy Spirit came upon them and they spoke with tongues and prophesied.'

Charismatics have been accused of dividing Christians into the 'haves' and 'have-nots', and on both sides there have at times been wrong attitudes. But it is an unavoidable fact that amongst Christians there are those who 'have' been baptized in the Holy Spirit and those who 'have not'. If this were not true the whole issue would be irrelevant. The question, 'Have you received the Holy Spirit *since* you believed?' is, however, extremely relevant.

Many Christians are afraid to let the Holy Spirit take control. They fear that surrendering to him will cause them to go to extremes. We need to realize that God can run our lives much better than we can! We need to see that God only gives good gifts unto his children (Lk 11:13). There is nothing to fear.

We need much more than frantic activity if we are to reach our world. Much of what is done in the name of God is unfruitful and fleshly. If we are to win men and women to Christ we need more than human wisdom and reasoning. 'For the kingdom of God is not in word, but in power' (1 Cor 4:20). The dynamite of God is able to destroy all man's arguments.

D. L. Moody speaking of the transformation that came to him after he was baptized in the Holy Spirit, said, 'One day in New York, Oh what a day! It is almost too sacred an experience to name. I can only say God revealed himself to me and I had such an experience of his love that I had to ask him to stay his hand. I went to preaching again. The sermons were not different, and yet hundreds were converted. I would not now be placed back where I was before that blessed experience if you could give me all the world.'

Moody also said, 'Now I believe the gift of the Holy Ghost that is spoken of is a gift for certain, but one that we have mislaid, overlooked and forgotten to seek for. If a man is only converted and we get him into the church, we think the work is done—and we let him go right off to sleep, instead of urging him to seek the gift of the Holy Ghost that he may be anointed for the work... The world would soon be converted if all such were baptized with the Holy Ghost.'

The baptism in the Holy Spirit not only transformed Moody's own life, but countless thousands of others who were saved through his ministry.

Something missing

After a wonderful conversion experience I longed to bring others into the new life that I had found. I read books on how to witness successfully and sought with all my might to share this new found faith. Yet it was as if my words bounced off those with whom I shared my faith without any real effectiveness. My attempts at spending time in God's word and in prayer fell far short of what I knew they should be. So often I found my mind was blocked or my thoughts wandered and although I wanted to pray, I just didn't know how or what to pray for. I knew there must be something missing because my life was so far removed from the Christian lifestyle I read of in the book of Acts. I felt I'd let God down.

One night I was feeling broken. I lay down on my bed with tears running down my face, grasping my Bible and saying, 'Lord could you ever use me? I think it would be best for both of us if you took me now. So I'm going to count to ten … and if I'm still here when I get to ten I'll know you want to use me and I'll live for you.'

'1, 2, 3, 4, 5, 6, (I counted more slowly now) 7, 8, 9,—(I hesitated) 10!' After a short pause I opened my eyes. I was still alive. Obviously God did want to use me.

A few days later I went to a meeting and although I couldn't remember a word the evangelist had spoken I knew I needed something, anything God would give me. So I shot forward when he gave an invitation for those to whom God had spoken to respond. As I shared my dilemma the counsellor asked me, 'Have you been baptized in the Holy Spirit?'

'What is that? I've never heard of it. But if God wants me to have it, I want it.'

As he prayed for me to be baptized in the Holy Spirit I knew something had happened, but I was not fully aware at that time of what a dynamic effect that night would have upon my life.

I soon found I had a new power in my witnessing. No longer was it just an 'outward commission' to witness, but an 'inward compulsion'. Within three days I led the first soul to Christ and within three more days he led his first soul to Christ. From then onwards I found I had a new ability to witness. My words had an anointing upon them I had never experienced before. People who had not previously taken any notice when I spoke to them were coming to the Lord now. I discovered a new ability and release in praise and worship. My staid, religious wineskin burst! I entered into a new dimension in prayer. Through the gift of tongues I could now pray beyond my understanding. When I ran out of words in English, I could switch into 'overdrive'. Because it was the Holy Spirit praying through me I could now pray right within the centre of God's will. I found a new closeness to the Lord and the fruit of the Spirit became much more evident in my life. But, that was just the start.

Don't stop

Acts 4 records how, as the disciples were praying that they might speak the word with boldness and that God would extend his hand to heal with signs and wonders, the place where they were gathering was shaken and they were all filled afresh with the Holy Spirit and spoke the word with boldness (Eph 5:18). Paul exhorted the Ephesian believers, do 'not be drunk with wine, in which is dissipation; but be filled with the Spirit.' The Greek word used here for being filled is in the present continuous tense. In other words 'be being filled' or 'continue to be filled' over and over. The baptism in the Spirit is not the end, merely a means to the end.

Sadly, many are as careful to avoid being filled with the Holy Spirit as they are to avoid being drunk with wine! Nevertheless, today we are experiencing a mighty outpouring of God's Holy Spirit. We are seeing God bring his people together even as he brought the dry bones together in Ezekiel's vision. However, we so need the 'breath' of God's Holy Spirit, if we are to be raised up a mighty army and reach our land for God.

Do you see your need of the empowering of the Holy Spirit?

'For the promise is to you and to your children, and to all who are afar off, as many as the Lord our God will call' (Acts 2:39). If you have been called by God, you qualify for the empowering of the Holy Spirit. How can you receive the Holy Spirit?

'Ask, and it will be given to you; seek and you will find, knock, and it will be opened to you. For everyone who asks receives, and he who seeks finds, and to him who knocks it will be opened. If a son asks for bread from any father among you, will he give him a stone? Or if he asks for a fish will he give him a serpent instead of a fish? Or if he asks for an egg, will he offer him a scorpion? If you then, being evil, know how to give good gifts to your children, how much more will your heavenly Father give the Holy Spirit to those who ask him?' (Lk 11:9–13).

You don't have to fear getting something bad! Ask! You may find it helpful to get someone who has been baptized in the Holy Spirit to pray with you. But Jesus promises *'Ask and you shall receive.'*

> The hand of the Lord came upon me and brought me out in the Spirit of the Lord, and set me down in the midst of the valley; and it was full of bones.
>
> Then he caused me to pass by them all around, and behold, there were very many in the open valley; and indeed they were very dry.
>
> And he said to me, 'Son of man, can these bones live?' So I answered, 'O Lord God, you know.'
>
> Again he said to me, 'Prophesy to these bones, and say to them, "O dry bones, hear the word of the Lord! Thus says the Lord God to these bones: Surely I will cause breath to enter into

you, and you shall live.

"I will put sinews on you and bring flesh upon you, cover you with skin and put breath in you; and you shall live. Then you shall know that I am the Lord'

So I prophesied as I was commanded; and as I prophesied, there was a noise, and suddenly a rattling; and the bones came together, bone to bone.

Indeed, as I looked, the sinews and the flesh came upon them, and the skin covered them over; but there was no breath in them.

Then he said to me Prophesy to the breath, prophesy, son of man, and say to the breath, 'Thus days the Lord God: "Come from the four winds, O breath, and breathe on these slain, that they may live.""'

So I prophesied as he commanded me, and breath came into them, and they lived, and stood upon their feet, an exceedingly great army.

Ezekiel 37:1–10.

5

Signing Up

Have you ever considered Jesus' methods of recruitment for his army?

Working hard by the Sea of Galilee were two fishermen, Simon Peter and his brother Andrew, casting their net into the sea. Jesus walked past them and just said, 'Follow me, and I will make you fishers of men' and continued to walk on. They were faced with a choice now. Either they were going to leave their business and their old way of life behind and follow Jesus or they were going to carry on as they always had. The Bible tells us 'they immediately left their nets and followed him'.

Next he passed two other brothers, James and John, mending their nets in a ship with their father Zebedee. Again he called them. They too were faced with a choice: they could say yes or no. Before, these self-employed fishermen had done what they wanted; from now onwards they had to surrender their wills to Jesus. 'Immediately they left the boat and their father and followed him' (Mt 4:18–22). That is the gospel of the kingdom. The kingdom of God on earth is revealed through a group of people whose King is the Lord. It is these God is raising up as an army, and he wants *you* to be a part of that army. But the choice is yours.

Many Christians have the attitude, 'The Scriptures do say

that there are vessels to honour and some to dishonour, I expect I'm one for dishonour.' However, this concept is based on a misinterpretation of Scripture. It is true that the Bible says, 'In a great house there are not only vessels of gold and silver, but also of wood and clay, some for honour and some for dishonour.' However, the decision as to whether you are a vessel to 'honour or dishonour' is not God's, but yours. The Bible goes on to say clearly in the next verse, 'Therefore, if anyone cleanses himself from these (sins), he will be a vessel for honour, sanctified and useful for the Master, prepared for every good work' (2 Tim 2:20, 21).

Jesus said, 'Follow me and I will make you fishers of men.' Notice that our responsibility is to follow him. When we follow him, he then takes the responsibility of making us into what he wants us to be: 'I will make you.' Jesus is not looking for great intellects or those with outstanding personalities, but rather, those who are willing to follow him obediently.

God himself has already decided he wants to use you. Will you sign up? His requirements? Everything!

1. Total commitment

To be used of God requires a total commitment. From now onwards your priority is your King and country—twenty-four hours a day, seven days a week. Many Christians want the best of both worlds. Seeking to gain the whole world, they lose their own soul. We do no one a favour by pressurizing them into becoming Christians, without explaining the cost. Becoming a Christian is far more than just having my sins forgiven so that I can be sure of heaven. To present this alone as the gospel is an insult to the King. Following Jesus means he now takes control and I live in obedience to him.

Lord (*Kurios*) is the most commonly used title for Jesus in the New Testament. Yet it seems in the evangelical church today that his most frequent title is Saviour. However, for every time that Jesus is called Saviour in the New Testament there are over twenty-seven references to him as Lord. The message of the gospel is not just 'accept Jesus as your Saviour', but let him be Lord in your life and he will save you. He doesn't want you merely to ask him into your life, he wants you to ask him in—to take over. He is King of kings and Lord of lords. He will accept one place in our lives: Lord and King. We come on his terms. We do not find the 'decision now, heaven later, do what you like in between, grace covers all' message in the word of God.

The rich young ruler is an example of someone who wanted to follow Jesus, but was not prepared for the cost. Wealth ruled his life and Jesus was not willing to share the throne with another. Although we read, 'Jesus loved him', Jesus' love would not allow him to lower his standard. It was all or nothing. The man went away sorrowful; when the choice was put before him his riches meant more to him than following Jesus.

It is not that there is anything wrong with having possessions, what is wrong is serving these things instead of using them to serve Jesus. Many Christians are seeking to have a foot in both kingdoms. They are fighting, but for the wrong things. They are fighting to hold onto their old way of life; fighting to get their own way. They pray, 'your kingdom come' but their actions say, 'My will be done.'

'No man that wars entangles himself with the affairs of this life, that he might please him who has chosen him to be a soldier.'

The Bible is clear, you 'cannot serve two masters'. 'Friendship with the world is emnity with God.' Divided loyalties make you God's enemy. He calls for total commitment. Yet many Christians run as soon as the going gets tough. In an earthly war, deserters are shot.

In the British Army when a recruit signs up, he wraps his civilian clothes in a parcel to send home. In doing so he is saying, 'I am making a break with my old life to serve Queen and country. No longer do I go where I want or do what I want.'

'If anyone comes to me and does not hate his father and mother, wife and children, brothers and sisters, yes, and his own life also, he cannot be my disciple. And whoever does not bear his cross and come after me cannot be my disciple' (Lk 14:26–27). Jesus' words are clear, 'He cannot be my disciple'! Commenting on this passage in his book *Discipleship* (published by Good News Crusade), Don Double explains that to 'hate' means, that our love for the Lord is so strong that our love for others in comparison looks like hate.

Cross bearing

The cross speaks of death. Someone once put it this way, 'Your cross is where your will and the will of God cross.' Are you willing to put on the altar those who are close to you, your reputation, your ministry, your possessions and make Jesus Lord of them? God has blessed us with many blessings but we need to see that we are only stewards and that Jesus is the true owner. He has offered us a wonderful life, there is nothing that can compare with living in the kingdom of God. But it costs everything to get that pearl of great price.

Abraham was faced with the ultimate challenge when he was called up to sacrifice Isaac, the most precious thing to him. His willingness clearly demonstrated where his heart was and therefore he did not have to carry through the full commission. Although he had already stretched out his hand and taken the knife to slay his son, God said, 'Do not lay your hand on the lad, or do anything to him, for now I know that you fear God, since you have not withheld your son, your only son, from me' (Gen 22:1–12). This was probably the greatest challenge of Abraham's life. In my own life when God has asked for things that were precious to me, sometimes it has got very close to bringing the knife down, and at other times it *has* meant bringing the knife down.

When people ask us, 'If I become a Christian, will it mean I'll have to stop…' it is so easy to reply, 'No, the gospel is free—there is nothing you can do to earn it.' However, although the gospel is free, we cannot enjoy fellowship with God and forgiveness, without being willing to submit to his lordship. Have you noticed how often Jesus put his finger on the thing that was central in a person's life? To the rich young ruler, it was his great possessions; to the Samaritan woman at the well it was her relationship with men. The fishermen were called to leave the family business and follow Jesus.

If Jesus were to allow compromise in the real issues in their lives, there would be compromise in every other area. Jesus never allowed compromise, but clearly spelt out the cost of following in a way that would discourage those who didn't really mean business. Had Jesus allowed the rich young ruler to follow him on his own terms, from then onwards whenever Jesus asked him to do something, an argument would have ensued, because his will was not surrendered to the Lord's. Were I to honestly look back over the years that I have walked with Jesus I would have no problem finding occasions where my obedience has been slow, following a time of conflict, rather than instant. God calls for us to surrender our will to him, however inconvenient, and, like Jesus, to say, 'Not my will, but thy will be done.'

I remember when God began dealing with me on this particular issue. I had claimed that he was Lord in my life and that everything I had belonged to him, yet, whenever God asked anything of me that seemed the slightest bit inconvenient, a minor battle began. One of the first areas God put his finger on was my car. 'You say your car is mine, and yet it's only insured for you to drive.' I gave my car to him: 'Lord it's yours, thank you for the privilege of letting me drive it.' That day I went around my home, giving the things I had to the Lord. 'I give you my cheque-book, it's yours, just tell me what figures to fill in.' 'I give you my stereo, it's yours Lord.' 'I give you my records, they become yours Lord.' That was fatal. Many of the records in my large record collection were ungodly. I knew that they had to go. If the record collection was now the Lord's it was he who should decide what to include in it, and I knew I had records he wouldn't want. That day a large selection of my record collection went down a local quarry…in pieces. 'Lord I give you my carpet, it's yours. Lord I give you my bed, it's yours. If on some occasion you need it for someone else, it's your bed.' Along with these went my ministry, ambitions, family and loved ones. Little did I know at that time that the Lord would take many of the things that were most precious to me. However, I also that day gave up the right to complain. I remember well, when I lost one of the most precious things in my life, sitting and sharing with a dear brother, tears running down my face. When suddenly I began to laugh, which quite surprised him. I turned and looked him in the eyes and said, 'When I gave that to the Lord, I never expected he would take it.'

This should not cause fear; God cares about us. He is not a tyrant. He wants us to have his best! Many times I have experienced how true the statement is that, 'The Lord only takes something away from us, because he's got something better.'

There is such a security in knowing that God wants his best for me, even more than I want it, and he knows what is best for me better than I do. This pearl may cost us everything, but, it is incomparable (Mt 13:46). Jesus promised, 'Assuredly, I say to you, there is no one who has left house or brothers or sisters, or father or mother or wife or children or lands, for my sake and the gospel's, who shall not receive a hundredfold *now in this time*, houses, brothers and sisters and mothers and children and lands, with persecution—*and* in the age to come, eternal life' (Mk 10:29–30).

You cannot lose!

In Britain we have a Queen. I have a great respect for her and am proud to have a monarchy in my country. However, in reality she has very little say in the decisions in our land. She is more of a figure head, for State occasions. The Government decides what happens. That is how many Christians view Jesus. 'You can forgive my sin because I don't want to go to hell, and you'll be nice for special occasions.' Sunday is the day when many Christians put on the biggest mask of the week. God hates that unreality. The Lord said, 'I'd rather you were cold than luke-warm' (see Rev 3:15). Their attitude is, 'You can be King, as long as I can be your government! As long as you don't start telling me what to do.'

A king in scripture was very different to an English monarch today. He was someone with great authority. *You didn't disobey the King twice*! We read that Esther even when coming before her husband, the King, came in fear and trembling, aware that 'whosoever shall come unto the king into the inner court, who is not *called*, there is one law of his to put him to *death*, except such to whom the King shall hold out the sceptre, that he may live' (Esther 4:11).

The Lord does not come to give us advice which we take or leave as we please. Jesus throws out the challenge: 'Why do you call me "Lord, Lord", and do not do the things which I say?' (Lk 6:46). The proof of his lordship in our lives is not our ability to sing choruses on the subject or preach about it, but that our lives are lived in obedience to him. Praise God we've been called! It is so good to realize, too, that God is patient. Yet let us not take God's goodness for granted.

A soldier risks being court-marshalled if he sends a message—'Tell the Sergeant Major, I don't feel like getting up today, I'm having a lie in.' Or, 'Tell the Sergeant Major, I'm not coming to the Parade today, I'm feeling too tired.' He has given up his own rights, to serve his King and country. Our call is: 'Seek first the Kingdom of God and his righteousness, and all these things shall be added to you' (Mt 6:33). The world seeks for nice property, clothing, food and transportation, but, saints, your 'Heavenly Father knows that you have need of these things' and as we seek first the kingdom of God and his righteousness in our lives, he will see that we have everything we need. The question is, what is our priority? Jesus is looking for an army willing to obey and submit to his will; soldiers who will unashamedly make a stand for him, twenty-four hours a day, seven days a week!

2. Make a stand

Paul proclaimed, 'I am not ashamed of the Gospel of Christ, for it is the power of God to salvation' (Rom 1:16) and, 'How shall they hear without a preacher?' (Rom 10:14). One of the first things I encourage new Christians to do, is to tell someone what has happened. I believe that to put into words however falteringly, what Jesus has done for you, seals it and brings an assurance with it. For, 'If you confess with your mouth the Lord Jesus and believe in your heart that God has raised him from the dead, you will be saved. For with the heart one believes to righteousness, and with the mouth confession is made to salvation' (Rom 10:9–10).

God does not call us to be secret Christians. We are not a secret service, but those who let our light shine in a dark world. The Christian's true citizenship is in heaven (Phil 3:20). On earth we are strangers and pilgrims. We are here as God's ambassadors. An ambassador is one who represents his country in a foreign land. God has sent us into the world as his representatives and our lives should be different to those of non-Christians.

Many Christians look on church as something tagged on to their lives and they feel that they are doing God a favour by going to one service a week. To go twice or attend a mid-week prayer meeting shows great commitment and spirituality. If we believe this, we have got it very wrong. Do you hide your light under a lampstand? Are you ashamed of Jesus? Are you embarrassed to stand up for him before non-Christians in your home, place of work or school? Jesus made it clear, 'Whoever is ashamed of me and my words, of him the Son of Man will be ashamed when he comes in his own glory, and in his Father's, and in the glory of the holy angels' (Lk 9:26).

It is so easy for us to say, 'We would lay down our lives for Jesus' and yet in reality we are not willing to live for him now. We say we would be willing to pay the ultimate sacrifice and yet in real life are so unwilling to make any sacrifice for the gospel. The story is told of a Vietcong guerrilla officer who said to a missionary in Vietnam, 'I would gladly die if I could advance the case of communism one more mile…as you have read to me from the Bible, I have come to believe that you Christians have a greater message than that of communism. But I believe that we are going to win the world, for Christianity means something to you, communism means everything to us.'

David Livingstone put it this way, 'I place no value on anything, except in its relation to the kingdom of God.' Can we say that?

Although we in the West have up to this time experienced little persecution, it may not always be so. In the Book of Acts when God was moving there was a revival or a riot and usually both together. Do we realize that in this century alone there have probably been more Christian martyrs than in the entire history of the Christian church? Throughout the world hundreds of thousands have died for their faith, especially in communist countries.

It is a fact that instead of hindering church growth, violent opposition has caused the church to grow. In the Book of Acts the persecuted Christians simply took the gospel with them wherever they were scattered. Persecution, misunderstanding and opposition may well come. The Scriptures make it clear that, 'All that would live godly lives in Christ Jesus shall suffer persecution.' The fear of offending a godless world or being unpopular has caused many in the West to settle back into a 'Sunday Christianity'. Somebody recently said to me, 'Christianity's all right as long as it doesn't affect your lifestyle.' A little bit of religion tacked on to our lifestyle offends few, but living the godly lifestyle God calls for, shows sin up for what it is and that is liable to offend those who have no desire to get right with God.

3. Instant obedience

Instant obedience is a key to victory. At the wedding in Cana Mary said to the servants, 'Whatever he says, do it' (Jn 2:5). This is an excellent example of instant obedience. Do you question Jesus' commands? Sometimes they may sound crazy.

Consider Gideon when God sent him to battle. After pruning his army down from 32,000 to a mere 300, he sent them out with trumpets, and flaming torches. To have charged the camp with swords would have been fatal and only have led to their destruction. Human initiative says, 'That's crazy', but, as they obeyed God, they won a tremendous battle without one casualty. Whenever God enters a battle he always wins. Before he sent Gideon's army to battle he got rid of the fearful and half-hearted. Today God is pruning the church to raise up a 'Gideon's Army', who will instantly obey his commands and go his way.

Consider also Jericho and the Israelites' mighty victory as they obeyed God. Can you visualize the reaction of Jericho's inhabitants as they watched Israel silently marching round their walls? Can you imagine the conversations within the walls? 'They must be mad, religious nuts.'

If we are to see territory taken for God we, his ambassadors, must obey him totally and instantly. When I first became a Christian the chorus, 'I have decided to follow Jesus no turning back, no turning back', was popular. Have you honestly prayed that prayer?

'Though none go with me, still I will follow, no turning back.
Where Jesus leads me, I'll surely follow, no turning back.
The cross before me, the world behind me, no turning back.'

Will you commit yourself totally to the King of kings and Lord of lords? Will you make a stand for him? Will you make it your priority to obey him? Christ is recruiting. He says to you, 'Follow me.'

'Lord I surrender to you, everything I have I give to you, I want you to be Lord. I want to serve my King and country. No turning back.'

That is signing up.

6

A Real Eye-Opener

The King of Syria had a problem. Somehow the information about his secret plans against the King of Israel was leaking out. He concluded that there must be a spy in the camp passing on information to his enemy. In a desperate bid, he sought to find out who the traitor was. To his surprise, the answer came back that it was God! He had been telling Elisha, his prophet, who in turn was warning the King of Israel (2 Kings 6:8–18). Regarding the prophet as a threat, he sent a great army to seize him. Elisha's servant was the first to see the approaching army and ran in fear to warn his master. Elisha's cool reply came as a surprise: 'Do not fear, for those who are with us are more than those who are with them' (6:16). It sounded crazy. As far as the servant was concerned he and Elisha stood alone against this vast army. So Elisha prayed—'Lord I pray, open his eyes that he may see.' Immediately the servant's eyes were opened, to see the mountains full of the hosts of God's army.

How we need God to open our eyes to the spiritual realm all around us. So often we see no further than the problems or oppression we feel.

Dead ducks

The story is told of a Negro slave who loved the Lord dearly and frequently talked to his master about the Lord and the battle against the devil. But his master would reply, 'The devil never bothers me.' One day while they were out together shooting duck, the master scored two hits. One of the ducks fell dead to the ground, the other lay flapping frantically trying to take off again. The servant quickly ran to collect the dead duck, but his master shouted after him, 'Don't go after the dead one, go for the one that's trying to fly off.' Suddenly it hit the servant. He turned and replied, 'Now I understand why you never get troubled by the devil.'

The devil hates the believer. He is more aware than we are that God has delegated his authority to the church and therefore it is the church that can spoil his plans. I believe it is impossible to have a living relationship with the Lord and not believe in the devil. I have heard so many Christians testify that when they found the Lord, they got to know the devil too. When Jesus set off on his mission after being filled with the Spirit, he soon encountered opposition. Christian, when you find your work for the Lord opposed, do not be surprised. We are involved in warfare!

The Scriptures frequently compare the Christian life with that of a soldier. Throughout the Bible warfare is a very common theme. Paul exhorted Timothy to 'Wage the good warfare' (1 Tim 1:18) and greeted Archippus as 'our fellow soldier' (Philem 2).

The early church recognized that their invisible enemy attacks everything good and wholesome: the moral, social, educational, judicial and spiritual life in their land. He is out to destroy:

(a) *Physically* with sickness and disease.

(b) *Emotionally* with depression, unhappiness and other spiritual maladies.

(c) *Mentally*, upsetting the mechanism in men's minds.

(d) *Morally* through pornography, adultery, lesbianism, fornication, homosexuality, etc.

Paul wrote, 'For we do not wrestle against flesh and blood, but against principalities, against powers, against the rulers of the darkness of this age, against spiritual hosts of wickedness in the heavenly places' (Eph 6:12). Our weapons are spiritual, as our enemy is.

For effective and victorious warfare, it is vital that we are aware that Jesus *has* disarmed the power of darkness. I was recently talking to a professional wrestler who told me that many of the fights he took part in had set scripts, with the winner decided before the fight ever began. We wrestle against principalities and powers and the world rulers of darkness, and God expects us to win every round! Satan may seek to put up a fight, but he is defeated. Before we enter the ring Satan knows he has to throw in the towel. Our wrestling is not to see who wins, but to take back for God territory that Satan is at present holding. However, today I see a major problem in our warfare against the kingdom of darkness.

What enemy?

There is a war on; we cannot be apathetic. Many have rewritten Ephesians 6:12 to read—'We wrestle not.' Even some so-called Christians hold the concept that Satan and his demon followers have either all died off, or are mere superstition. In our modern scientific age, many deny the reality of a personal devil or evil spirits and dismiss those who do as superstitious or unenlightened. However, a look at the box office hits these days reveals an interest in occult things. The promotion of disbelief in a personal devil is one of Satan's most successful tactics. For if you don't believe in Satan, you will blame God for the evil in the world: 'If there is a God of love why did he allow that to happen?' I believe that Satan has inspired the popular caricature of the devil as a funny red creature with horns and a pointed tail. Because of it most people have relegated Satan to the realm of fairy tales. It is only as our eyes are opened that we discover Satan's finger prints in our life and our world.

The Bible is clear that the devil is not just an evil influence nor 'the bad in men', but a personality created by God. Like man in the Garden of Eden he was created good and was also a free moral agent. He chose to rebel against God (Jn 8:44). Satan is a 'he' not an 'it' (Job 1:8; Job 2:1–2, Mt 12:26). In the Lord's Prayer, many translations have 'deliver us from evil' as though evil were a force. However in the original Greek it is 'deliver us from the evil one'. Evil is not a force but a person, represented by Satan, the evil one.

The devil and his angels have minds (Gen 3:1; Eph 6:11), emotions (Rev 12:12; Lk 8:31), memories and the will to act (Is 14:12–14). They will be punished as morally responsible beings (Mt 25:41; Rev 20:10). Jesus took Satan seriously, referring to him as 'the prince of this earth' (Jn 12:31) and 'the god of this world'. He is the one most people worship, although they are not aware of it.

In the preface to his book *The Screwtape Letters*, C. S. Lewis rightly says, 'There are two equal and opposite errors into which our race can fall about the devils. One is to disbelieve in their existence, the other is to believe, and to feel an excessive and unhealthy interest in them.' Although we have already seen that Satan is a defeated foe, we also need to realize that he is out to destroy us. When he loses the first round and his victim is saved, his next strategy is to seek to weaken the new Christian, rendering him powerless and ineffective in God's service. 'Be sober, be vigilant; because your adversary the devil walks about like a roaring lion seeking whom he may devour' (1 Pet 5:8). Don't be fooled, Satan hates you, and is out to make your life unproductive, unfruitful and defeated. Our minds, spirits, emotions and wills are Satan's targets. However, God has provided all the armour we need to 'stand firm' (Eph 6:10–20). It has been said, 'If you don't believe in the devil, try resisting him for twenty-four hours and you'll soon believe in him.' The Christian who begins to resist the devil becomes a threat. When we are all out for Jesus we become 'known' people. We are a threat to Satan's kingdom. Hell has a wanted poster up for us!

So many Christians are like the familiar cartoon character,

sitting comfortably in his armchair watching television totally oblivious to the fact that a battle is raging in his garden. While bombs explode all around him and tanks drive through his back yard, he continues to enjoy his favourite film. For too long indifference, apathy, fear of failure, prayerlessness and a lack of commitment has held back the church from making an impact on our land. Satan is happy to sit back and leave the church of God to its indifference and apathy, as in such a state little territory is taken and much is lost.

It is time to repent.

We desperately need God to open our eyes to see our calling, our inheritance, and the place of authority where Jesus is today seated. Isn't it amazing that the power which raised Christ from the dead is the same power which is both working in us and available to us as his church, called to exercise his authority in our everyday situations! If he is the head, and we are his body, and 'he has put all things under his feet', where does that leave Satan and his hordes? Someone once put it this way, 'If you want to know my shoe size, ask the devil.'

Every Christian is called for active service. There are no exceptions! In his first reference to the church Jesus said, 'The gates of hell shall not prevail against her.' It has been put this way: 'Either Satan is going to kick us around or we are going to kick him around.' Paul, writing to the saints at Rome, said, 'The God of peace will soon crush Satan under your feet'—whose feet—ours! Most Christians have no problem accepting that Satan is under Jesus' feet, but are totally unaware that God has delegated his authority to his church. He has called us to be overcomers (1 Jn 4:4): 'You are of God, little children, and have overcome them' (every spirit that does not confess Jesus Christ) 'because he who is in you is greater than he who is in the world.' It is vital we recognize our authority in Christ!

Delegated authority

When a person joins the Police Force he is vested with all the authority of the land. A nobody can find a new identity and becomes a somebody.

One night I was driving home from a meeting at which I had been speaking when I noticed a police car with a blue light flashing behind me. Realizing that he wanted me to stop, I pulled over to the side. It is not too unusual, late at night, to see people trying to get you to stop. But, as soon as I noticed this car, I realized if I didn't stop, I would be disobeying the law of the land. I was greeted by a young man who had lived for many years in the same town in which I had lived. I was unaware that he had joined the police force. A few years before he had been no one special, someone people didn't take much notice of, but now he had been delegated the authority of the law of the land. He was now different. In the same way, God has delegated to us the authority of his kingdom.

In Matthew 28:18, 19 Jesus appeared to his disciples saying, '*All* authority has been given to me in heaven and on earth, Go therefore....' Jesus is King with total authority and he says, 'I have all authority now I give it to you. Go on my behalf.' Jesus said, 'If you have faith as a mustard seed, you will say to this mountain, "Move from here to there," and it will move; and nothing will be impossible for you' (Mt 17:20).

Delegated authority is a fundamental kingdom principle. Satan wants the church to remain ignorant of its authority as he is aware that while Christians are ignorant of this fact, they can do little damage to him or his kingdom. However, a people truly aware of these truths can see ground taken for God. 'If God is for us, who can be against us?'

'Submit therefore to God. Resist the devil and he will flee from you.' Being in submission to God is vital if we are to exercise this authority. He has not given us authority just to have our own way, or do our own thing, but to see his purpose and will 'done on earth, as it is in heaven'. However,

God's word to every saint who will submit himself to God and resist the devil is 'He will flee from *you*.' From who? *You*!

Colossians 2:15 tells us that at the cross Jesus 'disarmed principalities and powers, he made a public spectacle of them, triumphing over them.' He won a total victory over his enemies. Now he has given us the authority to trample over all the power of the enemy unharmed (Lk 10:19).

It has been said that it is presumptuous for Christians to think they can stand against the powers of darkness when even the Archangel Michael himself dare not, but said, 'The Lord rebuke you' (Jude 9) to Satan. Were we the Archangel Michael, that would be true, it would be presumptuous to rebuke these powers. However, we are not. The Bible is clear that angels are 'ministers unto the heirs of salvation'. We are not angels. The Lord has dealt to the church an authority that they do not have. We rank higher than Satan and all of the angelic beings holy and fallen. This is not to depreciate the majesty of God's angels. However, the highest ranking angel is outranked by the most insignificant redeemed son of God. We have been elevated above all other created beings. No wonder Satan has sought to keep these truths hidden from Christians. In Jesus we have authority to rebuke the powers of darkness and render them ineffective, and then to loose situations and captives and set them free.

There are countless men and women who are bound and need releasing (Lk 4:18, 13:16). In Jesus' name we have authority to do this. When Jesus told us we should 'pray in his name' he was not issuing some magical formula to stick on to the end of our prayers to make them sound religious or let others know we are about to finish! When we pray in his name, we pray with his authority. We are acting in his stead as his representatives.

What's in a name?

When we speak in the name of Jesus, we speak as if he were there. When we pray in Jesus' name, we have the full backing of heaven. All of creation acknowledges Jesus and acknowledges, too, the ones to whom his authority has been delegated. When we pray in the name of Jesus it is as if he were doing the praying. How we need to see the importance of Jesus' name!

In the early church the believers preached 'In the name of Jesus'. In Jesus' name alone, people were saved (Acts 2:21). 'For there is no other name under heaven given among men by which we must be saved' (4:12). The sick were healed 'In Jesus name'. In the Book of Acts we do not find Christians praying for the sick, but commanding them to be healed and the sicknesses to leave in Jesus' name (4:29–30). The man lame for forty years was instantly healed when Peter spoke the words, 'In the name of Jesus Christ of Nazareth, rise up and walk' (3:6) and for the first time in his life he leapt, ran and walked. Demons were cast out 'In the name of Jesus' (16:18). Paul says, 'I command you in the name of Jesus Christ to come out of her', and the girl bound by demons was totally set free. Christians risked their lives and were willing to die for the name of Jesus (15:26, 21:13, 5:41).

So today, we are to 'do all in the name of the Lord Jesus' (Col 3:17). Let us realize that his name 'Is above every name' and 'At the name of Jesus every knee should bow, of those in heaven, and of those on earth, and of those under the earth' (Phil 2:9–10). At the name of Jesus every sickness, every bondage, and everything alien to the kingdom of God has to bow the knee.

That name has not lost any of its power or authority!

I believe we need to recapture a vision of the power in prayer, the urgency for prayer and our responsibility to pray.

The power in prayer

Prayer is not twisting God's arm to act in a way against his will. God is not reluctant. Neither is God helpless without man or less than almighty, but he has made the church his means of implementing Christ's victory over Satan. As John Wesley put it, 'God does nothing but in answer to prayer.' James tells us (4:2): 'You do not have because you do not ask.' Do we really believe, 'Prayer is where the action is' or is there still a lurking suspicion that prayer is a waste of time?

How we need God to open our eyes.

By prayer we can intervene in the affairs of the world and totally thwart Satan's plans. It is God's secret weapon. From your room you can score a direct hit in prayer, with amazing results, anywhere in the world and see Satanic strongholds broken.

God intends the church, not Satan, to be the controlling factor in human affairs. I believe the decisions that take place in our land are not made in the House of Commons nor the White House, but in the heavenlies. In prayer we have authority to deal with all activities opposed to the kingdom of God; to see laws changed, and ungodly laws not passed; to stand against the terrorism, cult activity, and sex shops that are invading our land. In Jesus' name, on numerous occasions, I have seen jobs open up for the unemployed where none were in sight. Many times we have used our authority in Christ over the elements, the wind, rain and snow.

Victories are won in prayer! 'The effective, fervent prayer of a righteous man avails much.' Elijah was a man with a nature like ours, and he prayed earnestly that it would not rain and it did not rain on the land for three years and six months! To the unenlightened observer the battle against Amalek was taking place in the field where they and Israel were in combat. However, the real battle was being fought and the victory won on the hill top where Moses, Aaron and Hur were interceding (Exod 17:8–11) for it was when Moses held up his hand that 'Israel prevailed' and when he let down his hand 'Amalek prevailed'. Israel was merely experiencing the results of the battle in the heavenlies being waged on the hill top.

When your prayers don't seem to be answered, don't give up. Jesus told a story of a man who received bread for his unexpected guests from his neighbours because of his importunity. The Amplified Bible captures the emphasis of the Greek of Luke 11:9 when it translates, 'Ask and keep on asking, and it shall be given to you; seek and keep on seeking, and you shall find; knock and keep on knocking, and the door shall be opened to you.' Don't give up. As it was once put, 'Units of prayer combined, like drops of water, make an ocean which defies resistance.' Time spent in prayer now, bears eternal fruit.

Urgency for prayer

If 'God does nothing but in answer to prayer' it should go without saying that prayer should be the top priority. Yet so often we are too busy with the cares and pleasures of this life to pray. God said, 'I sought for a man among them who would make a wall and stand in the gap before me…but I found none' (Ezek 22:30). If we are too busy to spend time in prayer, we are too busy.

The excuse 'I don't have time' is really invalid. We organize our time according to our priorities. If prayer is seen as a priority, we'll find time. Perhaps our priorities need re-evaluating. It may be that we need to reconsider the place of prayer in our church meetings. The Lord may provoke churches to start prayer cells of two or three in homes, early morning prayer meetings before work, all night or half nights of prayer, days of prayer and fasting or a prayer chain. Count Zinzendorf, the founder of the Moravians started a prayer chain which carried on day and night uninterrupted for a hundred years and led to the beginning of the missionary movement. The house-bound and elderly have not finished their usefulness, but can use their time to make intercessory prayer a priority. There is no retiring in the kingdom of God!

Our prayers are so often too general. Even if God did answer them, we wouldn't realize as they were so general. Let us seek God for specific burdens about which we can really pray.

Our responsibility to pray

If what we have seen is true about the power in prayer, and the urgency for prayer, we must be aware of our responsibility to pray. Samuel regarded it as *sin* if he neglected to pray for Israel. A look at church history clearly shows that prayer is essential for revival. Working and witnessing for the Lord are vital, but no substitute for prayer. It is irreplaceable. I believe that the future of our land rests in the hands of God's people. How we need to pray. Oh, what power! What urgency! What a responsibility!

Standing in the gap

God has given us tremendous authority in prayer. He looked for a man to stand in the gap so that he wouldn't destroy a disobedient people, but was unable to find one. God calls for us to be such people. So often we let doubt, laziness, and intellectual arguments stop us. Let us repent of our unbelief and apathy. When Christians hold up their hands in prayer, all the powers of darkness have to grind to a halt. '*The gates of hell shall not prevail against you*', does not just mean we will hold our ground, but that we will charge in and take over territory in the hands of the kingdom of darkness. In the ancient world the city walls were so thick that even houses were built into them. There was an outer gate and an inner gate for double protection, with a gap in between where the elders of the city would meet to oversee the affairs of their city and to plan for battle. This was referred to as meeting 'in the gates' (Deut 16:18; 21:19–20; 25:7; Ruth 4:11; Prov 31:23). All the elaborate plans and organized strategy of hell will not prevail against the church of God as she recognizes the authority delegated her by King Jesus. The prayer of faith can destroy in a few moments what Satan has been building up for years.

7

Taking Territory

God is a God of miracles. Creation was a miracle. The Bible is a record of God's miraculous dealings with mankind. His dealings with Israel were miraculous. Their deliverance from Egypt, crossing the Red Sea and being fed in the wilderness for forty years were amazing miracles! Jesus' birth, life, ministry, death, resurrection and ascension were all miracles! The transformation of the disciples from fearful failures to a mighty army who were turning the world 'back up the right way' after Pentecost was a miracle! Wherever they went miracles followed as the sick were healed, the dead raised and demons cast out! Every time someone is born again, a miracle takes place! Each answered prayer is a miracle! Our God has not changed.

A shaven Samson

Whenever miracles stopped, Israel lapsed into heathenism. God has placed within man a hunger for the supernatural. Take away the miraculous from Christianity and man is open to be deceived by the counterfeit supernatural events of our day. If we rob Christianity of the supernatural we are left with a 'sheared Samson'. Such a church will not have the delivering power God has planned us to have. Dead, formal religion will not have a drawing effect on our lost, sick, lonely, bound world. But where the Lord is meeting with the sick and healing them, the lonely are finding security and salvation, the bound being set free and the love of God is flowing, men and women will be drawn to Christ. Biblical evangelism is not just a proclamation, but also a demonstration. The gospel of the kingdom can be both seen and heard. Jesus came both '*preaching* and *showing* the glad tidings of the kingdom of God' (Lk 8:1). He came to destroy Satan's kingdom of fear, death, violence, hate, murder, lust, sickness and suffering.

'For this purpose the Son of God was manifested, that he might destroy the works of the devil' (1 Jn 3:8). The Greek word used here for 'destroy' (*luo*) basically means 'to come unglued, to loose or cause to lose consistence'. An example of this would be when the mortar of a building is rotten so that it begins crumbling and disintegrating. Everything Satan has built is breaking down! Each person who followed Jesus, each one healed and set free, was territory taken from Satan's crumbling kingdom. Jesus did not come to just 'save souls', but to save people, body, soul and spirit! The whole man. The gospel is not just words preached. Paul said, 'My speech and my preaching were *not* with persuasive words of human wisdom, but in *demonstration* of the Spirit and of power, that your faith should not be in the wisdom of men but in the power of God' (1 Cor 2:4–5).

When John the Baptist was having doubts about whether Jesus was the Messiah and sent some of his disciples to check up, saying, 'Are you the coming One, or do we look for another?' (Mt 11:2–3) Jesus didn't say, 'Take a copy of my last week's sermon notes for him to read.' Rather, he demonstrated his kingship. 'that very hour he cured many people of their infirmities, afflictions, and evil spirits: and to many who were blind he gave sight'. Then Jesus said, 'Go and tell John the things you have seen and heard: that the blind see, the lame walk, the lepers are cleansed, the deaf hear, the dead are raised, the poor have the gospel preached to them' (Lk 7:19–22).

Healing was a powerful part of Jesus' evangelism. It is not a 'side issue' as some would suggest, but took up a major part of Jesus' life and ministry. He 'went about all the cities and villages, teaching in their synagogues, preaching the gospel of the Kingdom and healing every sickness and every disease among the people' (Mt 9:35).

Why did a great multitude follow Jesus? 'Because they saw his signs which he performed on those who were diseased' (Jn 6:2). On hearing of Jesus healing a leper 'great multitudes came together to hear, and to be healed by him of their infirmities' (Lk 5:15). We are told that 'many believed in his name when they saw the signs which he did' (Jn 2:23).

'Jesus went about all Galilee, teaching in their synagogues, preaching the gospel of the Kingdom, and healing all kinds of sickness and all kinds of disease among the people. Then his fame went throughout all Syria; and they brought to him all sick people who were afflicted with various diseases and torments, and those who were demon-possessed, epileptics and paralytics, and he healed them. And great multitudes followed him—from Galilee and from Decapolis, Jerusalem, Judea and beyond the Jordan' (Mt 4:23–25). After the healing of the paralytic we are told that all who saw it 'were amazed and glorified God, saying, "we never saw anything like this!"' (Mk 2:12). After the blind man was healed we are told he followed Jesus glorifying God, and 'all the people, when they saw it gave praise to God' (Lk 18:43).

Miracles did not decrease when Jesus ascended back to heaven: rather they continued on an ever widening scale! For 'through the hands of the apostles many signs and wonders were done among the people…a multitude gathered from the surrounding cities to Jerusalem, bringing sick people and those who were tormented by unclean spirits, and they were *all* healed' (Acts 5:12, 16). Healing and deliverance are a vital and inescapable part of the gospel. When Philip went down to Samaria and 'preached Christ' to them, the result was that 'the multitudes *with one accord* heeded the things spoken by Philip, *hearing* and *seeing* the miracles which he did. For unclean spirits crying with a loud voice, came out of many who were possessed and many who were paralysed and lame were healed' (Acts 8:5–8). Their commission had not changed. 'Heal the sick, cleanse the lepers, raise the dead, cast out demons. Freely you have received, freely give' (Mt 10:8). At Iconium Paul and Barnabas stayed 'a long time, speaking boldly in the Lord, who was bearing witness to the word of his grace, granting signs and wonders to be done by their hands' (Acts 14:3). At Malta, the father of Publius, who was a leading citizen of the island, 'lay sick of a fever and dysentery'. Paul went in to him and laying his hands on him healed him. When this was done, the rest of those on the island who had diseases also came and were healed (Acts 28:8–9).

The name of Jesus was largely used in the healing of those who were not Christians. Someone once described it as 'God's method of advertising the ministry'. The disciples were sent to heal the sick and say to them, 'The Kingdom of Heaven is come near to you', not the other way round. 'Peter went down to the saints who dwelt in Lydda and found a certain man named Aeneas, who had been bedridden eight years and was paralysed. And he spoke the word, 'Aeneas, Jesus Christ heals you. Arise and make your bed.' The man immediately arose and all who dwelt at Lydda and Sharon saw him and turned to the Lord (Acts 9:32–35).

I do not believe that we will see a mighty turning to God without the 'signs following'. This is not because God is unable to do it any other way—he is sovereign. Rather, it is because the miraculous is an inseparable part of the gospel. Remove the miraculous and we are left with a dead, lifeless religion. Most of the people in our land believe that Jesus once lived, but is now dead and therefore has no real relevance to them today. They say, 'If Jesus is alive, why doesn't he do the same things he did 2000 years ago? If he's dead, he can't.' They are right. How we need to see a new demonstration of the kingdom in our streets and towns and villages. I believe this will be an important part of the mighty outpouring of God in our land. Testimonies of neighbours healed, will be the talking point on the streets.

It is alarming that in some countries the Christians attend church meetings on Sundays, but, when they are sick go to witch doctors, because the so-called 'fundamentalist' missionaries have said 'miracles are *not for today*'. During a crusade in Africa (the first in that town) I announced, 'Jesus is alive today! Mohammed is dead, Buddah is dead, but, Jesus is alive! But don't just take my word for it. He is going to prove it by healing the sick.' After I had preached the gospel, I said, 'I want every blind person to come forward.' As I spoke a blind beggar who was walking past overheard me. He hadn't heard the message, but shot forward before anyone else had a chance. In Jesus' name, he was instantly healed and started describing his surroundings excitedly saying, 'I can see'. I asked the crowd how many knew this man and knew that he had been blind and almost every hand was raised. After that other blind people came forward and were healed. Next I called for those who were deaf and that day every blind and every deaf person who came forward was instantly healed. At the end of the crusade we couldn't find one person who had been ministered to who had not been healed. No one had told them Jesus doesn't heal the sick today. So when I told them he does, they believed me!

God said it—that settles it!

God cannot lie. 'All the promises of God in him are "yes" and in him "Amen" to the glory of God' (2 Cor 1:20). Jesus made it clear, 'Heaven and earth will pass away, but my words will by no means pass away' (Mt 24:35). Yet so often unbelief robs us of the things God has promised. We let doubts invade our mind.

'What if it doesn't work?'

'But, that brother wasn't healed, so I might not be'.

Unbelief limits God's moving. Jesus in his own town 'did not do many mighty works there because of their unbelief' (Mt 13:58). There is an atmosphere of unbelief in our land and churches which is hindering our seeing a dynamic and supernatural move of God. God wants to deal with the unbelief in our hearts. We need to recognize that unbelief is sin. Unbelief calls God a liar. It says, 'I know that you've said you'd do these things in your word, but I don't believe you will'. There is only one answer for sin and that is repentance.

The major thing that held me back from taking a step of faith was the nagging doubt, 'What if nothing happens?' Until I decided, 'Even if nothing happens, I've still been obedient to Jesus' commission.' After that, on a number of occasions I offered to pray for friends when they were sick and although some declined, others accepted my invitation and were healed (and later saved). What would happen if they had not been healed? My pride would have been hurt!

Where are the Elijahs?

How we need leaders in our land, who dare to stand up and say, 'If the Lord is God, follow him, but if Baal then follow him…. The God who answers by fire, he is God' (1 Kings 18:21, 24). Elijah knew his God and despite the false prophets' failure and cries for their god to 'baal' them out, he poured water over the sacrifice, drenching the wood and sacrifice and filling the trench around the altar. Then he simply said, 'Lord God of Abraham, Isaac and Israel, let it be known this day that *you are God* in Israel, and that I am your servant, and that I have done all these things at your word. Hear me, O Lord, hear me, that this people may know that you are the Lord God and that you have turned their hearts back to you.' Then the fire of God fell, consuming not only the burnt sacrifice, but also the wood, stones, dust and water! On seeing it the people fell on their faces, saying 'The Lord he is God! The Lord he is God!' (1 Kings 18:25–39). This was not an act of presumption on Elijah's part, but the action of a man who knew his God. Where are the Elijahs today who will show up the false prophets around us for what they are? Miracles should be a natural part of church life (Gal 3:5; 2 Cor 12:12; Jas 5:14–15).

He wants to use you!

In recent days God has been preparing the church for the task which is ahead. However, the big question is, 'Are we ready?' It may be some comfort to remember, that it was immediately after rebuking his disciples for their unbelief and hardness of heart that Jesus commissioned them to, 'Go into all the world and preach the gospel to every creature', promising 'These signs will follow those who believe: in my name they will cast out demons; they will speak with new tongues, they will take up serpents; and if they drink anything deadly, it will by no means hurt them; they will lay hands on the sick, and they will recover' (Mk 16:14–18). Then he 'was received up into heaven, and sat down at the right hand of God' (16:19). He could sit down with full authority on the throne!

The disciples then went out, with Jesus' delegated authority, to continue what he had begun. They preached everywhere and, 'The Lord worked *with* them and confirming the word through the accompanying signs' (16:20). Isn't it tremendous to realize that we are not called to just work 'for' God but 'with' him (2 Cor 6:1)? Almighty God has actually given us the privilege of being partners with him (Mk 16:14–20), of being his 'fellow workers' (1 Cor 3:9). As we have already said, this is not because he is incapable of doing the work on his own, but because he wants us to work 'with him'. In the New Testament, when God 'confirmed the words with signs following' everyone knew who was speaking! As the disciples went about, the Lord was bearing witness to what they said, 'both with signs and wonders, with various miracles, and gifts of the Holy Spirit' (Heb 2:4). Jesus has not changed. He is the same *today* and *forever* as he was yesterday! (Heb 13:8). I believe that today signs *should* follow 'them that believe'. When I preach the Word of God I expect to see it confirmed. It is God saying, 'I agree with what you said.' Jesus now lives in us (Gal 2:20; Eph 3:17; Col 1:27; 2 Cor 13:5) and plans to continue what he began through us!

Anyone for table tennis?

So often we play unspiritual 'table tennis'. God says, 'I have given you authority to do this' and we pray, 'Lord, you do it.' When God gives us a job to do, we so often just knock the ball back into his court.

The Lord says, 'Lay hands on the sick and they will recover' and we pray from a distance, 'Lord lay your healing hand on that sick person.'

The Lord says of believers, 'They will cast out demons in my name' and we pray, 'Lord that person needs setting free, set them free Lord.'

We pray, 'Lord, that brother really needs you to train him and shape his life.' Jesus says, 'Go and make disciples.'

We pray, 'Lord, care for these new Christians.' Jesus says, 'Shepherd my sheep.'

So often we are like Gideon who prayed, 'O my Lord, if the Lord is with us why then has all this happened to us and where are all his miracles which our fathers told us about, saying, "did not the Lord bring us up from Egypt?" But now the Lord has forsaken us and delivered us into the hand of the Midianites' (Judg 6:13). It was true that God did lead his people out of Egypt; however Moses was his instrument. God parted the Red Sea, but if Moses had not held his rod over the waters, they would have stayed closed because this was the way God had chosen for the miracle to take place. It is true that God caused water to come from the rock, but only when Moses hit it.

The Lord's reply to Gideon was somewhat of a surprise: 'Go in this your strength and deliver Israel from the hand of Midian. Have I not sent *you*?' God was saying, 'Yes I can deliver your nation from the hand of Midian, but I will use you as my instrument to do it.'

The Lord has not called his saints just to be spectators but to be actively involved in the things he is doing. Jesus said, 'These signs will follow those who believe: in my name they will cast out demons; they will speak with new tongues; they will take up serpents; and if they drink anything deadly it will by no means hurt them, they will lay hands on the sick, and they will recover.' We are then told that after the Lord Jesus had spoken to them, 'he was received up into heaven and sat down at the right hand of God and *they* went out and preached everywhere, the Lord working *with* them and confirming the word through the accompanying signs.' Jesus is seated at the right hand of God, with total authority, but he has delegated his authority to us. We have been called to 'reign in life through the one, Jesus Christ' (Rom 5:17). Our reigning will not just begin when Christ returns, but we reign now 'in life'. We have been given authority to deal with all activity opposed to the kingdom of God. Christians who know their authority in Christ are the most influential people on earth.

We need to recognize that Satan is a squatter! A squatter is someone who takes up residence in or on someone else's property and refuses to leave. This is God's world and God has given us a legal eviction order drawn up in the court of heaven and signed in Jesus' name. We have been given the right and authority in Christ to evict Satan and his hoardes from God's property. We are now called to execute that eviction as God's representatives on earth!

That is Good News!

8

...And Now for the Good News

The word gospel means 'good news'. It was the term used in ancient times for a runner who brought the news of victory at battle.

'How beautiful upon the mountains are the feet of him who brings good news, who proclaims peace, who brings glad tidings of good things, who proclaims salvation, who says to Zion, Your God reigns!' (Is 52:7). We have good news to share—there has been a battle, and Jesus has won!

Our God reigns!

At the cross the total penalty and full consequences of sin were laid on Jesus. All the sin, sorrow, suffering, pain, poverty and disease of mankind (Is 53:4–5; Pet 2:24). Why? So we should have to bear the weight of them too? No. From Genesis to Revelation there are thousands of promises concerning God's provision for all we need, body, soul and spirit, both now and for eternity. Jesus bore our sin so that we do not have to! There is no sickness, bondage or poverty in heaven. God's world-wide purpose and call for us is a total elimination of sin and its consequences. To pray, 'Your will be done, on earth as it is in heaven' (Mt 6:10) is to pray for the total abolition of these things here and now. We have been blessed with 'every spiritual blessing in the heavenly places' (Eph 1:3), yet we live like paupers. Accounts of old people dying in poverty, leaving large amounts of money hoarded away, are common. In the same way, many Christians live in poverty, unaware that in Jesus they are rich.

The prince and the pauper

The story is told of a king and queen many years ago who were bringing home their newborn prince from the royal hospital, when their carriage collided with a pauper's cart, coming from the midwife's house in the other direction. In the ensuing confusion the couples picked up the wrong babies. So the prince had to solicit on the streets for food unaware that the very streets on which he begged belonged to him! They were the property of his true father. Often he would walk to the palace gates to watch the little boy as he played. He would think wistfully, 'If only I were a prince.' He was a prince, the heir to the throne, but he didn't know it!

We are kings!

All the benefits that Jesus won on the cross are ours! Yet so often we live in poverty. Let us consider some of the results of Christ's victory.

(a) *Victory over sickness*

'Jesus went about all the cities and villages, teaching in their synagogues, preaching the gospel of the Kingdom, and healing *every* sickness and *every* disease among the people' (Mt 9:35).

'His fame went throughout all Syria, and they brought to him all sick people who were afflicted with various diseases and torments, those who were demon-possessed, epileptics and paralytics, and *he healed them*' (Mt 4:24).

'Great multitudes followed him, and he healed them *all*' (Mt 12:15).

'When evening had come, they brought to him many who were demon-possessed. And he cast out the spirits with a word, and healed *all* who were sick' (Mt 8:16).

Have you noticed that *all* who came to Jesus in faith were totally and completely healed. Yet many Christians believe that sickness is something which we have to live with. At best they hope that it will soon go away. Many say, 'If Jesus were around today I know I would be healed.' This reveals that they have failed to see why he ascended into heaven and poured out the Holy Spirit. His plan was not that there be fewer miracles, but more! He said of all believers, 'They will lay hands on the sick and they will recover' (Mk 16:18).

You don't have to go to the Middle East to be healed, but can be made whole right where you are now! Were miracles any less frequent after the Lord ascended and poured out the Holy Spirit? No. Acts 5:16 tells us 'a multitude gathered from the surrounding cities to Jerusalem, bringing sick people and those who were tormented by unclean spirits and they were *all* healed.' For 'Through the hands of the apostles many signs and wonders were done among the people' (Acts 5:12).

Satan will attack saints with sickness in the same way that he will tempt them. However, would you say, 'It must be God's will for me to sin, otherwise he would not have allowed me to be tempted'? I believe you would resist the temptation, fully aware of its source. The Scriptures make it clear where sickness comes from (Job 2:7; Lk 13:10–17; Acts 10:38). Yet so many Christians passively accept all that Satan piles on to them. After Jesus was anointed with the Holy Spirit he went about 'doing good and healing *all* who were oppressed by the devil, for God was with him' (Acts 10:38). Now we have been anointed with the Holy Spirit, he plans to continue through us what he began.

'Bless the Lord, O my soul, and forget not all his benefits; who forgives *all* your iniquities, who heals *all* your diseases' (Ps 103:2–3). If you are going to preach that God will only heal some sicknesses, you had better preach that he will only forgive some sins. It is the same 'all' in both contexts. Healing is one of the benefits which are ours through the cross. I do not pretend to understand why everyone prayed for is not healed instantly. I have found unbelief, fear, past occult involvement and deliberate sin, resentment and anger to be common blockages; ultimately, though, one has to ask God that question. (The subject is covered in greater depth in Don Double's book *After the Prayer of Faith* published by Good News Crusade.) We pray, 'Your kingdom come, your will be done, on earth as it is in heaven' (Mt 6:10). Sickness is not God's will. There is no sickness in heaven (Rev 21:4). You may be enjoying kingdom life in your spirit, but Jesus wants to bring it into your body and soul too. It is God's will that 'You may prosper in all things and *be in health, just* as your soul prospers' (3 Jn 2).

God is on the side of health! Living in health is better than being healed. Christ bore our sicknesses so that we don't have to bear them (Mt 8:17). 'He *has* born our diseases and carried our pains' (Is 53:4 Lit. Hebrew, and 1 Pet 2:24). By Jesus' stripes 'you *were* healed' (1 Pet 2:24). Notice that the verbs are in the past tense. I know I can come and receive God's forgiveness because he bore my sin. In the same way, I know I can receive his healing and wholeness because he bore my sickness. Today, if you are sick, 'be healed in Jesus' name'.

(b) *Victory over fear*

I have seen many hundreds permanently set free from fear in the name of Jesus. 'God has not given us a spirit of fear, but of power and of love and of a sound mind' (2 Tim 1:7). The two do not mix. Fear robs us of a sound mind and if God has not given us a spirit of fear, guess who has! Satan wants to bind us and rob us of our freedom in Christ. The only fear we should have is a fear (that means 'a healthy respect for') of the Lord (Ps 111:10). Yet fears of the dark, making mistakes, closed or open spaces, heights, death, sickness, old age, failure, cats, dogs and other animals and insects, to name but a few, bind many. God has given us dominion over the animals, yet to fear them means the animals have dominion over us. This of course does not mean we put ourselves deliberately in a place of danger or try God out 'to see if it works'. However, I have experienced God's protection on a number of occasions when I have been unable to avoid certain dangerous situations.

Some years ago God had to set me free from a fear of spiders. The liberty God had given me had ample opportunity to be tested while I was ministering in Africa, having big black spiders crawling round my bed at night. I remember turning to Nigel, the missionary I was with, and saying, 'Which are the poisonous ones?' To which he replied, 'I don't know, I can't tell the difference.' I learned, in a new way in that situation, to bind Satan's power and go straight into a peaceful sleep, claiming the truth of Mark 16—'They will take up serpents and if they drink anything deadly it will by no means hurt them.' I slept under God's protection. The Lord wants to set us free.

How often we miss God's best because we say, 'There are others far worse.' That may well be true, but with Christ's healing and wholeness it is not a choice between you or another. There is provision for all! There may be those 'far worse' but what of that! Jesus wants to set *you* free too! What a tremendous testimony in a world full of fear, to be able to say, 'I was frightened of that, too, but Jesus has set me free.' The psalmist David, pursued by those seeking to kill him, knew the freedom that comes from casting our cares on the Lord. He could say, 'I sought the Lord, and he heard me, and delivered me from *all* my fears' (Ps 34:4).

All means all. *In Jesus' name* you can be set free, right now!

(c) *Victory over the power of darkness*

All around us there are people bound in different areas of their lives. Those bondages vary from fear, depression because of persistent habits, right up to a total take-over by demonic powers. They all need to be set free. The Scriptures do not teach that deliverance is a specialist ministry, but the responsibility of all believers (Mk 16:17). It is part of the gospel which we have been called to proclaim. We have been given 'power over unclean spirits, to cast them out, and to heal all kinds of sickness and all kinds of disease' (Mt 10:1). We are called to 'set the captives free'.

Jesus said, 'These signs will follow those who believe: in my name they will cast out demons' (Mk 16:17). Notice how this is the first thing the Scriptures mention when they describe what the believers are doing. The book of Revelation goes on to record how the saints overcame Satan's forces 'by the blood of the Lamb and by the word of their testimony' (Rev 12:11). Satan hates the blood, for by it he was totally defeated! We will consider this area in greater depth in the following chapter.

(d) *Victory over death*

Fear of death is something which grips mankind. During one of his shows David Frost once asked the audience how many feared death. Almost everyone admitted that they did, though their reasons varied. For some it was the finality of death. For others it was the fear of the unknown. What was beyond death? Where would they go? For others, it was because they had a good idea where they would be going!

Jesus, however, came that through his death, 'He might destroy him who had the power of death, that is, the devil, and release those who through fear of death were all their lifetime subject to bondage' (Heb 2:14–15). He came to set us free from the fear of death and to bring us eternal life. Eternal life begins now and will never end! Jesus has taken the 'sting' out of death. A bee which has lost its sting can harm no one. It could cause fear to the one who was unaware that it had lost its sting, but the fear would be unnecessary! For the Christian, death is neither the end nor a mystery; it is a certainty of spending the rest of eternity with Jesus. He has promised never to leave you or forsake you. For the Christian, death is but the doorway into the full presence of God! Death is to be 'absent from the body and to be present with the Lord' (2 Cor 5:8). The psalmist tells us, 'Precious in the sight of the Lord, is the death of his saints' (Ps 116:15). Paul could say, 'For to me to live is Christ, and *to die is gain*. But if I live on in the flesh, this will mean fruit from my labour; yet what I shall choose I cannot tell. For I am *hard pressed* between the two, having a desire to depart and *be with Christ*, which is far better. Nevertheless to remain in the flesh is more needful for you' (Phil 1:21–24). Christian, there is no need to fear death, it is not the end, but rather graduation! God's army is unique in that its troops can die or be killed and still enjoy promotion!

(e) *Victory over hurts and rejection*

I believe that it is hard to live in our society these days without being hurt and rejected. There are examples all around us: those neglected by their parents; those who have prodigal children; those abandoned by their marriage partners. Some were abused as children. Many feel that they were failures at school, or they are now unemployed and feeling useless. Then there are the victims of broken homes and those suffering from the after effects of an unhappy love affair. Many have been told they are useless, or ugly, and have accepted these labels. These things get a grip on a person's life and frequently stop them reaching their full potential in Christ. The childhood reply to those who said unkind and cruel things: 'Sticks and stones can break my bones, but words will never hurt me' is not true. Words deeply wound and injure people. Many wish they had never been born or believe the devil's lie, 'You'll never make any-thing in life.' So they never try. It's a lie! You are special. When God made you he *didn't* make a mistake!

Much of my life, both before and after I was saved, was motivated by a desire to be wanted and accepted. It was not until the Lord set me free, that I began to really discover who I was. After that I could honestly say, 'Thank You, Father, for making me, me.' Many try to hide their hurt with jokes, drink, pills or even a religious facade. The old saying, 'time heals' sounds good, but time doesn't heal, rather it tends to magnify the hurt, so that the slightest provoking causes pain. Only God can heal the hurt. For some rejection manifests itself in an inability to give or receive love. They clam up when any physical contact is made. Others go to the opposite extreme and are constantly seeking affection, attention and approval, always looking to see what other people think of them.

Jesus came to heal broken hearts and set us free. He knew what it was to be rejected. 'He is despised and rejected by men, a man of sorrows and acquainted with grief, and we hid, as it were, our faces from him' (Is 53:3). He was rejected by his family who said, 'You are mad, come home', rejected by the religious leaders of his day. Even his friends all ran and left him when he needed them most. That was painful enough. However, on the cross, as he bore our sin, even his Father, with whom he had known perfect fellowship from eternity past, turned his back on Jesus, causing him to cry out, 'My God, my God, why have you forsaken me?' (Mt 27:46). Jesus knew what rejection was. He was despised, so you can be set free—set free from the hurt deep down inside, set free from an inferiority complex, set free to begin building deep, honest relationships. You can be healed of those hurts and set free, in Jesus' name...right now!

9

How to Get Bound

We have been called to set the captives free.

A friend of mine had a vision of Lazarus hopping out of the tomb, with new life but still bound up in the grave clothes. The Lord turned to the people and said, 'Loose him' (Jn 11:38–44). However, the people were themselves bound and they hopped around trying to unwrap Lazarus without effect. To set others free, we must ourselves be free. Many Christians are alive, but there are still areas where they are bound and need setting free.

Every so often the newspaper headlines tell how a prisoner's comrades have aided his escape. They have set free a captive—in this case, someone who shouldn't be free. Jesus came, however, to set free those who were captive, who shouldn't be bound. Our commission from him is to set captives free.

The dictionary defines liberty as 'the right and power to do as one pleases'. When a person is powerless to do things he wants to do, or feels compelled to do things he does not want to do, then we would say that he is 'in bondage'. A captive is someone who is imprisoned and unable to escape and therefore needs to be delivered or set free.

Jesus is King

The message of the kingdom is that Jesus is King. He is Lord of all, with *all* authority. Every knee must bow to the name of King Jesus. We have considered how during the time he walked on earth he was constantly setting people free from the things Satan had put upon them. Wherever Jesus went sinners were receiving God's forgiveness, the sick were being healed and demons leaving their captives. The kingdom of God was being established. Jesus was taking over territory that Satan had held in people's lives. Where Satan had brought bondage, Jesus brought freedom. Where Satan had inflicted sickness, Jesus brought health. Where Satan brought death, Jesus brought life. Where Satan had brought condemnation, Jesus brought forgiveness. He said that, 'The Spirit of the Lord is upon me, because he has anointed me to preach the gospel to the poor. He has sent me to heal the broken hearted, to preach *deliverance to the captives* and re-covery of sight to the blind, to *set at liberty those who are oppressed*, to preach the acceptable year of the Lord' (Lk 4:18–19). Jesus can set people permanently free, for, 'If the Son makes you free, you shall be free indeed' (Jn 8:36). When we talk of Satan binding people's lives, many immediately think of such people as the Gadarene demoniac, living among the tombs, breaking in pieces the fetters and chains with which men tried to bind him, crying out and cutting himself with stones (Mk 5:1–15). However, the Scriptures also tell us of a man in the synagogue who had an unclean spirit. It implies that he was an outwardly normal man attending a religious meeting. It is reasonable to suppose that he was a regular attender at the synagogue, and yet he too needed setting free.

Many are held prisoner, gripped by compulsive sin and habits, yet unaware that they are bound and need loosing. Others have been placed in psychiatric hospitals receiving electric shock or drug treatment, whose real need is for Jesus to set them free. (I am not suggesting that all those in psychiatric hospitals are demonically bound, for some their need is for physical or emotional healing.)

Much discussion has taken place as to whether a person is 'possessed', 'suppressed' or 'oppressed' causing much confusion. However, in the Greek we find no such distinction. The Bible simply talks of people having a demon. The Greek word is *daimonizomai*, literally 'demonized'. The same word is used of the Gadarene demoniac and the man in the Temple. The important thing is not how the man is bound, but that he can be set free.

This whole area of deliverance was one that I once avoided like the plague. To be honest, the idea of people being bound by demons repulsed me.[1] I loved praying for the sick and it was thrilling seeing them healed. But the thought of setting people free from demons and risking the possibility of people starting to scream, convulse or foam at the mouth, roll on the floor and things like that, which often happened when Jesus set people free, had caused me to avoid this realm (Mk 1:25; Lk 9:37–41).[2]

One of my first encounters in this area, was when a young lady, who was known to be suicidal, was brought to hear me at an evangelistic rally and sought to come forward and worship me. Completely thrown by the situation, I called for the stewards to remove her. This was something I did not wish to get involved in, so I tried to forget it.

A few weeks later a normal-looking girl attended a meeting. As she sat through the meeting I felt a real concern in my heart and an uneasiness in my spirit. Later that night, after returning to the home I was staying at, I was burdened to

[1] The subject of deliverance has caused fear in some which has been made worse by tragic stories in the newspaper of attempts at deliverance by those who were usually unsaved and often involved in open sins and immorality, totally unaware of the powers they were dealing with. Acts 19:13–17 tells of the seven sons of the Jewish Chief Priest who sought to cast out demons when not in a right relationship with the Lord: they were attacked by the possessed man. This serves as a warning for those who regard it all as a game. This is not an area for enthusiastic amateurs. Our authority comes out of a continual relationship with God. We also need to have a clear understanding of what the word of God has to say on the subject.

[2] Although certain manifestations do sometimes occur when people are set free, we should not go looking for them, nor do I believe that they are

pray for her and as I did, I felt such a presence of evil around me. I began to pray in tongues and rebuked Satan. A feeling of peace came to me and I fell asleep. The next day she turned up again at the meeting and after it had finished continued to sit on the front row. I went up to one of my colleagues and said, 'There's something wrong with that girl, will you have a word with her and find out what's the matter?' Then it all came out. Her mother had been a spiritualist and she too had got involved in it, thinking it was innocent, and had become gripped. She said that at times she was overcome by an evil power and she rolled up her sleeves revealing hundreds of lacerations to her arms; she explained that when she was overpowered she would take a razor and cut her arms in shreds. We prayed with her and she was completely set free in Jesus' name.

On a later occasion I was preaching at a Bible school. As I began to pray with the students who had come forward for ministry, one of the girls began to scream out and pushed back in fear. She cried out, in a very gruff masculine voice, that seemed to come from the pit of her stomach, 'I know who you are, you've come to destroy us.' Immediately I commanded the demon to be silent and took her to a side room with the Principal of the College and one of her girl friends. When she got into the room she confessed that she had been involved in lesbianism and that it had got a grip on her life. After she had repented of this sin, we were able to set her free in Jesus' name. The transformation in this girl's life was amazing. Her face, which had earlier looked tormented, was now radiant with joy.[3]

---

necessary for a person to be set free. Demons, knowing they are defeated, will draw as much attention to themselves as they are allowed to. It is usually a ploy to frighten and distract people. Satan is a showman. Jesus did not enter into conversation with the demons. When they spoke he rebuked them saying, 'Be quiet and come out' (Lk 4:34–35). He 'did not allow the demons to speak' (Mk 1:25–34; Lk 4:41).

[3] I've heard it said that lesbians and homosexuals are 'sick' and that we just have to 'love them' rather than seeing them as sinners who need to be set free from satanic bondage. But I have seen many lesbians and homosexuals set free in Jesus' name.

Up until this time I had deliberately sought to avoid the area of deliverance, regarding it as controversial and feeling it might ruin my reputation, but after seeing so many bound people, and the change in their lives when they had been set free, I knew that I could avoid it no longer.

Linda had been brought to my meeting by friends who hoped she might find some answers to her problems. She was a very attractive young girl but stood out because of her glassy stare. Later, as I was praying for the sick, she ran to the front screaming, 'Jesus is dead, I know. I was there. I saw him die.' The stewards came forward to restrain her, but this petite young girl just pushed them away with unnatural strength. Addressing the unclean spirits that bound her I spoke out, 'Be quiet, I rebuke you in Jesus' name and command you to leave her and never return. In Jesus' name, go.' The girl fell flat on to the ground and for a few seconds lay there motionless. Later she shared how her grandfather was a spiritualist and that she had got into bondage by playing with an ouija board at College. At times she would feel overpowered and say and do things against her will. But now she was free![4]

The Scriptures tell us clearly that we should 'not be ignorant of Satan's devices'. It would be crazy for soldiers to battle against an enemy, if they neither knew who he was, nor the tactics he employed. Satan is fully aware that Christians are the only ones who have an answer to the bondage into which he has brought men and women.

Fear not

This subject always causes a reaction, usually either an obsession or fear. Although we need to recognize Satan's tactics, let us not become obsessed with the subject, nor become fearful: 'Greater is he that is in us than he (Satan) that is in the world.' Satan is defeated. 'Fear not little chil-

[4] We do not have to go looking for demons. Jesus never did. Where there is the presence of the Lord and the anointing of the Holy Spirit they cannot hide.

dren, it is your Father's good pleasure to give you the kingdom' (Lk 12:32). The names 'Satan' and 'devil' are only used twice each in the book of Acts, and they are not compliments! 'God anointed Jesus of Nazareth with the Holy Spirit and with power who went about doing good and healing all who were oppressed by the devil' (Acts 10:38). Jesus has 'disarmed principalities and powers' and 'made a public spectacle of them triumphing over them' at the cross (Col 2:15). Now, having 'all things under His feet', he is head over all (Eph 1:22) with 'all authority' in heaven and on earth (Mt 28:18). Satan cannot touch your life, unless you let him. However, there is no place for complacency. 'Submit to God, resist the devil and he will flee from you' (Jas 4:7). We are 'to be on the alert, be sober, be vigilant; because your adversary the devil walks about like a roaring lion seeking whom he may devour' (1 Pet 5:8).

Under God's umbrella

The story is told of a man who went to his pastor and asked the question, 'Pastor, can a Christian have a demon?' to which the pastor replied, 'It depends what he wants to do with it.'

I am aware that the question, 'Can Christians be bound?' has caused much controversy within the church. However, after praying for many hundreds of Christians to be set free, I have concluded that to deny this ministry would be to rob many of the opportunity to be set free.

Christian, be aware, Satan is out to ruin your life and make you ineffective and unfruitful for God. However, while you are under God's covering he cannot touch you. We have already seen that Jesus had 'all authority' (Mt 28:18) and therefore the only authority Satan can now have, is that which we give him. The Bible is clear that when we submit ourselves to Christ and resist the devil, he has no choice but to flee. In Christ there is protection. To submit yourself to Christ means to put yourself under his rule. Christ's covering is like an umbrella; while I stay under the umbrella, in submission to him, I remain dry when it rains. However, if I rebel against him and come out from under his protection I risk getting wet. Proverbs 1:33 says, 'Whoever listens to me will dwell safely, and will be secure without fear of evil.' *God's purpose is for believers to oppress demons not the demons oppress the believers.*

There are, of course, people obsessed with demons, hunting for them everywhere and blaming them for everything, including human error, sins of the flesh and laziness. In doing so, they have glorified our defeated foe, seeking to cast out demons when the real need is for repentance, obedience to God and self-control. You can't cast out the flesh! To the person who says that they need to be set free from a lying demon and a spirit of stealing, Paul's words are very relevant—stop lying, and stop stealing (Eph 4:25,28). That is not to deny that there are those who, despite a real desire and willingness to stop, find themselves unable to and need setting free. For many others the real need is for the healing of emotional hurts. It would be outside the scope of this book to deal at length with the subject of the discernment of spirits. Suffice it to say that the gift of insight to see the source of the trouble is available to the Spirit-filled Christian. It is interesting to note that Paul at Philippi did not instantly cast the demons out of the possessed girl who followed him, but allowed her to continue for 'many days' (Acts 16:18), waiting for the right moment.

Psalm 91 talks of resting under the shadow of the Almighty, our refuge and our fortress. God is our fortress and while we are in that fortress we are secure. The devil can't touch you unless you go out. The Bible tells us that we are 'hidden with Christ in God' (Col 3:3). What safer place could there be? Satan requires our consent to gain an entrance. 1 Timothy 4:1 tells us about those who departed from the faith and gave heed to seducing spirits. That is how Satan could 'fill' the hearts of the two disciples Ananias and Sapphira (Acts 5). The teaching that 'Now you are a Christian Satan cannot touch you', is only part of the truth. The Bible teaches clearly that we should not 'give place to the devil' (Eph 4:27). The fact that God has given us this warning makes it clear that it is possible to give Satan a place. The Greek word for place is *topos* meaning a 'region' or 'area of land'. It is possible to let Satan get a foothold in some area of our lives. Although some Christians find instant deliverances when they give their life to Christ, it would be unrealistic to suggest that this is always the case. Many Christians are bound and need setting free.

Jesus died to make you a whole person and if you now realize that there is an area of your life where you are a captive, you can be set free. Paul talked of those who had become shipwrecked, whom he had handed over to Satan that they might learn not to blaspheme (1 Tim 1:20). Another brother in the Lord had, because of immorality, been delivered over 'to Satan for the destruction of the flesh, that his spirit might be saved in the day of the Lord Jesus' (1 Cor 5:5). I have had to pray for many hundreds of Christians to be set free because they had given place to the devil by coming out from under Christ's covering and protection.

There are many who need setting free from the 'snare of the devil, having been taken captive by him, at his will' (2 Tim 2:23–26). It is not my purpose here to try to convince the sceptic, but to help those who find themselves oppressed and to warn others. Prevention is better than cure. When God puts up a sign saying, 'Do not touch', it is very dangerous to touch. To suggest that we can do so, unharmed, is as ridiculous as to suggest that a soldier can freely walk into enemy territory when he wishes without being taken captive. Let us then consider how to get bound.

How to get bound

(a) *Indulgence in forbidden activities*

To deliberately indulge in forbidden activity such as immorality, rebellion, perversion, continual criticism and resentment opens the door to Satan. We are called to yield our whole being to God (Rom 6:12–14). If I yield my 'members as instruments of unrighteousness unto sin,' I give the enemy a foothold. People indulge in sin to begin with because it is pleasurable, yet once they have opened the door to sin it soon gets a grip on their lives. When people begin smoking they do not intend to become enslaved by it but they soon find that they cannot break the habit. The same is true of such things as drunkenness, drug use and pornography. The thing they considered was under their control, ended up controlling them. Others, who gave place to anger outbursts, have later found that the smallest of irritations would cause them to erupt violently. If someone does something that upsets me there are a number of things I can do. I can obey the Scriptural command to 'not let the sun go down on your wrath' (Eph 4:26) and make sure that before the day is out I have forgiven and if possible put it right with the one involved. Or I can harbour the hurt and continually mull it over, which only magnifies the situation so it looks far worse than it really is and bitterness against that person begins to grow in my heart until it grips me.

After a meeting in America, a man came and shared with me that he had no joy of salvation. As we began to talk it became clear that there was bitterness in his life. He opened up and shared that since the war with Japan he had grown so resentful that whenever he saw someone from that country, although it was now years later, it still made him physically sick. As he forgave, speaking out as if his enemies had been there, 'I forgive you,' he began to weep and weep and was completely set free. This tough man hugged me and sobbed as he experienced release, and explained how he had become hardened and not cried in years.

Others have indulged in immorality and lust only to find when they wanted to stop that it had got a grip on their life. It has even driven some to rape and murder.

To yield your will is to open the door (Rom 6:16). 'Whoever has no rule over his own spirit is like a city broken down, without walls' (Prov 25:28). When Germany invaded Russia in 1941 there was a cartoon put out showing Adolf Hitler being embraced by a massive bear. The caption read, 'I've caught a bear but he won't let me go.'

Satan seeks to deceive Christians into thinking they can backslide, and can always come back to God when they feel like it. Judas may be an example of such a man. As treasurer of the money given to Jesus he began putting his hand in the purse and stealing the money. No doubt it had small beginnings. Possibly he thought, 'No one will know what I'm doing, I'm getting away with it.' However, as he continued to do it, he opened the door until we read in Luke 22:3 'Satan entered Judas.' The end result was Judas' betrayal of Jesus and subsequent suicide.

Jesus was tempted but he never let Satan get any grip on his life at all. Temptation is not sin. However, when the temptation comes, it is our choice whether we reject that temptation outright or begin to meditate upon it. The person who begins to harbour it soon finds his defences are broken down and ends up like a city without walls. When Jericho's walls fell down the Israelites were able to enter that city and destroy their enemies. Until they fell, there was no means of entrance. When we yield our members as instruments to God, he is our Master and we have his protection. However, if we yield ourselves to sin, sin becomes our master, and seeks to enslave us.

(b) *Hereditary*

Scripture speaks of the sins of the father being visited on the children to the third and fourth generation (Exod 20:5). On a number of occasions I have known people to be bound as a result of their parents' or close relatives' involvement in either the cults or the occult, especially if they were subjected to such activities. One young man who came to me for ministry shared how his mother had been an epileptic, though he had not. Yet when his mother died he had instantly become an epileptic. After he had been prayed for in the name of Jesus and set free, he never again had a fit. (This is not to say that demon possession is synonymous with epilepsy, the Bible clearly distinguishes between the two. On this occasion the mother's fits had been an outward manifestation of a demonic grip which had come into her life through occult involvement. On her death the demon had entered into her son who at that time had not been a Christian.)

(c) *Cult practices*

Dissatisfaction with a lifeless church has led many into searching for reality in the cults and the occult. Sadly Satan and power-seeking men have offered a wide variety of traps. Jesus clearly warned that false prophets would arise to deceive. Many of the cults in our land today seem extremely friendly and often use what seems like Christian terminology. Some even quote from the Bible (cf 2 Cor 11:14). However, let us not be deceived. The Bible calls their teachings 'doctrines of demons' (1 Tim 4:1). (No prizes for guessing who inspired them!) These cults usually deny one or all of the fundamental Christian doctrines, such as Christ's divinity, the virgin birth, his substitionary death, bodily resurrection, the divinity of the Holy Spirit (relegating him to being a force, an 'it') and a literal heaven and hell. They usually teach that there are other ways to God than through Jesus, for example, through good works, and they supplement the Bible with other books or writings, claiming that the Bible is not sufficient alone. Also they demand intensive supervision and indoctrination (commonly known as brainwashing) and a break with all family ties, even lying and denying their true identity in order to deceive. To open yourself up to such heresy is to open yourself up to Satan.

You may have tried sharing the Lord with members of the Jehovahs Witnesses, Mormons, Christian Science, Divine Light Mission, Scientology, Hare Krishna, Bahai Faith, Christadelphians, Moonies or members of other sects, but however clearly you present the gospel it seems that they just do not see what you are saying. This is because Satan has a grip over their mind. Many Christians stand for hours arguing with them, but getting nowhere, regarding the cults' teachings as purely false doctrines, unaware that Satan has gripped the minds of their adherents. Unless they are willing to hear the truth and receive Christ it is a waste of time and the Christians open themselves to error. Jesus warned 'false christs and false prophets will arise and show great signs and wonders, so as to deceive, if possible, even the elect' (Mt 24:24). When encountering those involved with the occult and cultish activities we need to recognize that our battle is not against flesh and blood, man's theories or theology, but against the principalities and powers behind them who have 'blinded their minds' so that without a divine revelation they are unable to hear what we are saying. Clever arguments are not enough.

We need also to realize that the members of other world religions are not just worshipping false gods, but that when men bow down to idols, the demons behind their idolatry accept the worship (1 Cor 10:20,21). Satan desires worship. Sacrificing to idols is sacrificing to demons, not to God. It is Satan who has propagated the lie that all religions of the world lead men to the same God. The Bible is clear that there is only one way to God and that is through Jesus and to worship anyone but him is in fact worshipping the devil (Rev 9:20; Deut 32:17).

However, let us not just relegate these 'doctrines of demons' to the cults. Sadly many of these satanic lies are being taught in so-called 'Christian churches' in our land today and many Christians are actively supporting them, hoping that God might move there! Membership of a recognized Christian denomination does not instantly make a local church scripturally sound. The church is not a true church if its members explain away the Scriptures, openly permit sin, compromise God's word and indulge in pious and lifeless religious 'worship'. We should not align ourselves with such a group without a very clear call from God. It is not sufficient simply to desire to see God working in the church or to wish to reach out in love. Membership of such a church makes us prime targets for Satan's attacks and renders us vulnerable to deception and spiritual aridity.

(d) *Occult activity*

There is a real hunger for reality in our land and where the church has been slack, Satan has not. A world that is seeking for God and the supernatural has sadly been allowed to move towards the occult by a church which for too long, has either not made a stand against Satan's activities (some ministers even encourage the use of such things as spiritism, Yoga, hypnotism, fortune tellers and make their buildings available for such practices) or has denied the supernatural as 'not for today'. Dispensationalist teaching, that miracles and the gifts of the Spirit passed away with the last of the apostles, has been responsible for many serious seekers after God getting ensnared by Satan, whose counterfeits have offered them more than just words! There is an interest in the supernatural which is fed by such films as *The Exorcist*, *The Omen* and a glut of films and books on the supernatural, science fiction, witchcraft and other occult subjects. To deny that there is reality in them would be foolish. Let us not be deceived. They are not all 'tricks'; sadly, many are real. The satanic magicians (Exod 9:10) could copy many of the miracles which God performed through Moses and Aaron. The Bible reveals two sources of supernatural power: God and Satan (Rev 13:13–14; Acts 8:9–11). The miracle of Aaron's rod turning into a serpent before Pharaoh's eyes was counterfeited by his magicians. However, Aaron's serpent swallowed up the others. Let us remember, Jesus is Lord!

Any occult participation, regardless of the degrees of involvement, is an open invitation to the powers of darkness and involves forfeiting divine protection. This is the main avenue Satan uses to bind his victims. I remember one woman who, before becoming a Christian, had crippling back pains which, after weeks of agony, led her to go to a spiritist healer. Following that visit she appeared to be well and the pain left. However, on becoming a Christian, the pain instantly returned. Satan does not have creative power like God, he can only do a cover-up job, a counterfeit to the real thing. The story did not end there. After she had repented of her sin in going to a spiritist healer, she was healed in the name of Jesus.

As a young lad I had unsightly warts on my right wrist. Despite the application of various liquids which the doctor had given me to remove them and attempts at burning them off, they did not go. In desperation I went to a spiritist who was involved in wart charming, a visit which was totally unfruitful for the warts remained. Years later, after becoming a Christian and hearing that Jesus could heal the sick, I went forward at a meeting. However, the warts were not healed. That night, on returning from the meeting, I suddenly remembered going to this spiritist and turned to a brother who was with me and asked, 'Do you think this could be a hindrance to my being healed?' He said that he firmly believed it could and so we prayed together and I asked for forgiveness. The next morning when I woke up, there was not a wart left on my arm!

Although a lot of occult practices have proved to be phony, the Scriptures give the direst of warnings against any dabbling with the occult. (Ezek 13:17–23; Gal 5:19–22; Acts 8:9–24; Acts 13:8–12; Acts 19:13–20; Lev 19:31; Lev 20:6–7; Deut 18:10–13; Is 8:19–20; Rev 22:14–15; Rev 21:8; Lev 20:27; Exod 22:18; sorcery was punishable by death.) I believe it is impossible to indulge in occult practices, however mildly, without in some way being affected.[5] In his book *Roaring Lion* (published by the Overseas Missionary Fellowship), Robert Peterson writes about his encounters with spiritism while he was a missionary in Borneo:

I have asked several sorcerers who have been willing to talk to me about the circumstances of their becoming witchdoctors. In every case it started with illness, in seeking healing through the use of magic as prescribed by a sorcerer, they opened the way for a demon to possess them. Not every one who uses magic when ill becomes possessed. However some develop serious psychic disturbances and become obsessed if not possessed. Others later suffer from chronic sickness, fear, compulsive thoughts and behaviour, suicidal tendencies, emotional instability, severe depression and an inability to comprehend truth. (Most do not realize the connection between their condition and the occult involvement until it is pointed out.) I have not come across a

[5] For a more detailed study of these areas, I recommend *Cults and the Occult Today* by Forrest and Sanderson (Marshall, Morgan & Scott).

single case where people have been involved in spiritism without there being a distinct deterioration of physical, mental or spiritual faculties.

Yet spiritism often hides under a guise of being 'religious' and sometimes even claims to be 'christian spiritualism'. These two words are incompatible. Deuteronomy 18 gives us a clear warning against such activities (18:9–14).

Curiosity killed the cat

In Deuteronomy chapter eighteen the Lord gives his people a stern warning: '*When you come into the land which the Lord your God is giving you, you shall not learn to follow the abominations of those nations. There shall not be found among you anyone who makes his son or his daughter pass through the fire* (walking on hot coals and through fire is one satanic manifestation in some eastern religions) *or one who practises witchcraft, or a soothsayer, or one who interprets omens.*'

Included in this category are such things as fortune telling, palmistry, astrology, ouija boards, tarot cards, clairvoyance, crystal balls, ESP (Extra Sensory Perception), telepathy, horoscopes and automatic writing. Many claim to have 'psychic powers' which are required for fortune telling or mind reading. However, this is just a counterfeit name for what the Bible describes as demon possession. Most occult activities have been regarded as 'harmless fun' entered into 'just for a laugh'. Such things as levitation, ouija boards, and tarot cards are often indulged in as fun at school and college parties and even sold as children's games! Most daily papers and magazines carry horoscopes. However, in almost every case I have come across, those few moments of 'harmless fun' have ended up leaving people bound.

Hypnotism has become highly popular and is being widely advertised as a cure for illnesses and smoking and a means of bringing increased prosperity or confidence. Even in the medical profession some are using it as a supposed cure, seeking to justify this ancient practice. I believe this to be one of the most dangerous occult activities today. To 'open your mind', to let go of your control over yourself, opens the door wide to demonic powers to take control. Claims of crimes committed and embarrassing and immoral acts carried out, while people were under hypnosis, have been made. We should never surrender our minds and wills to anyone but Jesus and even then we are still in full control. We should never surrender the right to say yes or no. Accounts of people under hypnosis talking of their past life as someone else (reincarnation) merely show that people have opened their minds to Satan's deceptions. The teaching on reincarnation has taken literally thousands to hell. These people believed that they would end up in some spirit world or come back in some other form, but the Bible has made it clear that: 'It is appointed for men to die *once*, but after this the judgment' (Heb 9:27). Teaching on reincarnation is one of Satan's key tools for deceiving people into thinking they are all right. It stops people facing the fact that they will go to hell if they don't accept Christ as their Lord and Saviour, here and now.

Yoga is an extremely popular practice today, even among some Christians. We need to see that its origins are firmly rooted in Eastern mysticism and although it involves physical contortions, it is primarily not physical. On many occasions I have found that those who have got involved in Yoga simply for the physical 'benefits' have ended up either getting hooked on eastern religions, or finding themselves spiritually bound, unable to hear God and comprehend spiritual truths and often oppressed by moodiness and depression.

I believe that horoscopes are a major door into deeper occult activity. It is said that one third of British adults read their horoscopes, unaware that such things are sin and an abomination to God. Those involved in writing the horoscopes are usually deeply involved in the occult (Lev 19: 26–31). The abominable practice of astrology has become 'respectable'. Many business men make their decisions from consultations with an 'observer of times'. Most people who seek to observe the times through such means as horoscopes, fortune telling, etc., regard it as 'innocent fun', until Satan eventually sees that the prediction comes true, causing them to become dependent on reading their horoscopes before they dare to do anything. By indulging in any of these occult things, they provide Satan with the worship he desires. God made it clear that it is an abomination to seek guidance from anyone but him and for such sin his judgement comes upon the nations who do those things.

'*Or a sorcerer, or one who conjures spells*' Most people visualize a witch as a fairy tale old woman astride a broomstick. However, we must not be blind. Witchcraft is very common in our land. After a meeting a lady came forward who seemed fairly normal and I was amazed when she shared how she wanted to be set free as she was a practising witch. After she had repented the Lord instantly set her free.

One farmer came to a meeting who used water divining to locate blocked drains in his fields. He was not convinced when my colleague, Michael Darwood, and I told him that such activities were wrong. However, being a Christian, he agreed to let us pray that if this activity was not of God, the next time he tried it, it would not work. The next day he came back and burnt his divining sticks, seeking God's forgiveness for playing with satanic things. He went home freed in Jesus' name and aware beyond doubt that dowsing has nothing to do with 'magnetic forces' attracting the rods. (This is supported by the fact that some hold them over maps of sites to reveal water sources.) However the story did not end there: that night as he slept, the Lord showed him a map of the farm with all the drains marked and told him he knew where the drains were better than Satan did.

We never lose out by obeying the Lord!

'*Or a medium, or a spiritist, or one who calls up the dead*' One of Satan's main goals is to deceive people into believing that on death everyone goes to some spirit world, where they all live 'happily ever after'. He most certainly does not want them to believe that they will spend eternity in hell if they do not receive Christ. Spiritualism is Satan's major tool in pro-pounding this lie. After a visit to a medium they say, 'It must be Uncle Albert who I was talking to, he talked of how he used to tap his pipe on the fireplace and no one but his close relatives would know such a thing.'

The powers behind the seances are demonic and dangerous. God slew Saul in battle for consulting a medium (1 Chron 10:13–14). Satan and his demon followers know more about the departed friend or relative than we do. That is why the Bible (Is 8:19) refers to them as 'familiar spirits'. The demons are familiar with the voice and information and seek to impersonate them to deceive (Lev 20:27). They are far better impersonators than Mike Yarwood. The unsuspecting relative is convinced that it is their deceased loved one they are talking to and get further entrapped.

Sightings of unidentified flying objects (UFO's) are common today. In cases where no natural explanations can be found I believe that such things are not aliens from other planets but either angels or demons. It is interesting to note that studies carried out on those who claim to have sighted UFO's indicate that very often the observers have in some way been involved in occult activities. They have thus made themselves vulnerable to Satan's lies and deceptions. Satan is the master of 'lying signs and wonders' (2 Thess 2:9) and the Bible warns of signs in the heavens. This is no new manifestation. Right back in the book of Genesis we read of evil 'beings from the spirit world' coming down to earth and even having sexual relationships with human women (Gen 6:1–4 TLB). The idea that houses are haunted by the 'ghosts' of departed people is another deceptive lie of Satan. I have come across houses where a satanic grip, as a result of past evil activities, has revealed itself. In Jesus' name this grip has been broken.

'For all who do these things are an abomination to the Lord, and because of these abominations the Lord your God drives them out from before you' (Deut 18:9–14). The Bible is clear that all such activities are sin and an abomination to the Lord for which his judgement will come upon the nations (Mal 3:5; Deut 18:12).

During my years in the ministry I have discovered that the main barrier to people coming through into the fullness of the Spirit and receiving the gifts of the Spirit, has been past occult activities. When seeking to move into the fullness of God's kingdom, we need to repent and renounce all past activities connected with the kingdom of Satan. I have found, too, that people who have a fear of God's supernatural works have usually been frightened by some past encounter with the occult.

I would like to close this chapter with a warning and a promise.

Keep well away from all occult practices. To come out from under Christ's rule puts you in a very vulnerable and dangerous place. However, if you have indulged in any of these things in the past you can find freedom in Jesus.

Satan is a defeated foe and Jesus Christ is Lord! Those who will repent of such activities and turn their life over to him can experience complete liberty, for Jesus came to set the captives free.

10

How to Be Set Free

In chapter 9 we considered how someone gets bound. Now let us look together at how they can be set free.

(a) *Recognize*

If you are bound, you need to see where you opened the door, to ask God's forgiveness for opening it and to go back and close the door. In other words to *recognize* you are bound, to *repent* of sin involved and to *renounce* all contact with the area of bondage.

(b) *Repent*

Repentance is foundational in entering the kingdom of God. From the start John the Baptist came preaching, '*Repent*, for the kingdom of heaven is at hand' (Mt 3:2). Jesus' message, too, was, '*Repent*, for the kingdom of heaven is at hand' (Mt 4:17). In answer to his convicted hearers' question on the day of Pentecost, 'What shall we do?' Peter replied, '*Repent*, and let every one of you be baptized in the name of Jesus Christ for the remission of sins; and you shall receive the gift of the Holy Spirit' (Acts 2:38).

The word 'Repent' implies a change of mind and purpose for the good, and is translated from a Greek military term which means 'about face', a 180 degree change in direction.

(Greek—*metanoeo*.) The change of mind is the result of seeing what our sin did to Jesus. Repentance is not just a feeling of sorrow, but a willingness to stop and go in the opposite direction. In the past we were going our own way, doing whatever we wished, now we have turned and are going God's way. The things we once loved, we now hate.

Repentance is necessary because it is sin that gives place to the enemy. Although people are bound, they are still responsible for their own sin. Any sin which opened the door to the bondage needs to be repented of, however 'innocently' it may have been entered into. I have on many occasions known people set completely free after true repentance.

When Jesus arrived at Gadara a man possessed by demons ran and fell on his knees in front of him (Lk 8:26–39). Despite the extent of bondage, he was still able to make a positive response to the Lord. He bowed the knee to King Jesus. This is vital when someone wishes to be set free. The spokesman demon said its name was Legion 'for we are many'. A Roman legion consisted of five to six thousand soldiers! Yet the man still responded to Jesus! Jesus did not engage in a lengthy 'deliverance session', nor in the naming of each demon, but by a word he cast them out. I believe the key was the man's desire to be set free and his willingness to turn from sin. A demon can only bind a person for as long as he is given the right, but when that area of life is submitted to Christ, and the devil is resisted, he has no option but to flee.

I get concerned when I hear accounts of hours and hours and even days spent in deliverance sessions. I would suggest that the person bound wasn't willing to admit his sin, and to come into the light and submit himself to Christ. Jesus cast out the demons with a word—not even a sentence! I have seen many people, from those who have dabbled with the ouija board and horoscopes, right down to witches, set free in seconds, when they have been willing to honestly come into the light concerning their sin and renounce it. On occasions, when freedom has not immediately come, I have been aware that I could spend hours battling, but have stopped and said to the person, 'Unless you are willing to be honest and renounce the sin that got you into this mess, I'd be doing you an injustice to set you free.'

Jesus instructed a man, 'You have been made well. Sin no more, lest a worse thing comes upon you' (Jn 5:14).

We do no one a favour by setting them free unless they are willing to surrender to Christ. In fact, the Bible clearly warns that, 'When an unclean spirit goes out of a man he goes through dry places, seeking rest and finds none. Then he says, 'I will return to my house from which I came,' and when he comes, he finds it empty, swept, and put in order. Then he goes and takes with him seven other spirits more wicked than himself, and they enter and dwell there; and the *last state of that man is worse than the first*' (Mt 12:43–45).

(c) *Renounce*

Finally there needs to be a total breaking with the sin that led to the bondage and a severing of the effects. When Ephesus received the gospel, 'Many who believed came, confessing and telling their deeds. Also, many of those who had practised magic brought their books together and burned them in the sight of all. And they counted up the value of them, and it totalled fifty thousand pieces of silver. So the word of the Lord grew mightily and prevailed' (Acts 19:18–19).

Does this sound 'too extreme' or 'too radical'? I believe that a total break is vital if the word of God is to grow and mightily prevail in our lives and area. I've seen literally thousands of pounds worth of occult equipment, tarot cards, ouija boards, lucky charms and shelves full of occult books go up in flames as people have renounced these things and made a break. There is a need to get rid of all that Satan would seek to use to keep a grip on you, regardless of the cost! Only a true repentance and renouncing closes the door and brings victory.

Occult involvement is often known to affect people physically (sickness), mentally (most often by fear and depression) and *always* spiritually (Mt 6:24). But the effect of the bondage can be broken and severed in Jesus' name.

In conclusion

If you *recognize* that you are bound, or have had any sort of contact with a cult or occult practices, you need right now to:

Repent, recognizing it as sin, however ignorant you were at the time. Then—*renounce* all contact with the sin, destroying anything necessary, severing any effects of the sin.

Then, '*In Jesus' name, be totally set free.*'

Aftercare

If you are to stand firm it is now vital that you commit yourself to a caring body of Christians who can stand with you and build you up in the word of God. Also, be filled with the Holy Spirit and practise godly discipline.

You are now free to obey and live for King Jesus.

> In the name of Jesus,
> In the name of Jesus,
> We have the victory,
> In the name of Jesus,
> In the name of Jesus,
> Demons will have to flee,
> Who can tell what God can do?
> Who can tell of his love for you?
> In the name of Jesus, Jesus
> We have the victory.

11

Praise God

Following the outpouring of the Holy Spirit at Pentecost, Peter had to explain to the crowd, 'These are not drunk, *as you suppose*, since it is only the third hour of the day. This is what was spoken by the prophet Joel' (Acts 2:15–16). Can you imagine being asked by outsiders as you are walking from your Sunday morning service, 'Are you all drunk?' For too long Christians have been regarded by the world as a bunch of staid negative people, whose theme song is 'Thou shalt not'! Many a child has gone seeking life in the world because the local church their parents attended was so lifeless and compromising that it brought no challenge to stir them to serve the Lord.

Exuberance and spontaneity characterized the first century church's worship. The early Christians stood out because of their excitement about the fact that Jesus is Lord. The world needs to see the life and excitement that should be radiating from the church. Many Christians regard praise and worship as unimportant, a 'side issue' or even a waste of time. However, a glimpse into heaven reveals the priority given to praise and worship. David, too, recognized how important praise is and set aside a vast army of four thousand Levites for the sole purpose of praising the Lord (1 Chron 23:5).

He exhorted:

'Shout joyfully to the Lord, all the earth; break forth in song, rejoice, and sing praises. Sing to the Lord with the harp, with the harp and the sound of a psalm, with trumpets and the sound of a horn; shout joyfully before the Lord, the King' (Ps 98:4–6).

Praise and worship are the natural outcome of seeing the King. David made a commitment:

'I will bless the Lord at *all times*, his praise shall *continually* be in my mouth. My soul shall make its boast in the Lord; the humble shall hear of it and be glad. Oh, magnify the Lord with me, and let us exalt his name together' (Ps 34:1–3).

Praise and worship are *not* a side issue!

Let us consider together some reasons why we are to praise God.

(a) *Because the Lord commands us to*

Praise and worship are the language of the kingdom of God. We are 'A chosen generation, a royal priesthood, a holy nation, his own special people.' Why? 'That you may proclaim the praises of him who called you out of darkness into his marvellous light' (1 Pet 2:9).

We are commanded, 'in everything give thanks' (1 Thess 5:18) and told, '*whatever you* do in word or deed do all in the name of our Lord Jesus, giving thanks to God the Father through him' (Col 3:17).

Praise and worship are not just Sunday activities! 'This *is* the day which the Lord has made, we will rejoice and be glad in it' (Ps 118:24). If the Lord made the day, how can we grumble about it?

'Clap your hands all you peoples, shout to God with the voice of triumph' (Ps 47·1) This is not a suggestion, but a command. It is common to hear people say, 'I praise God my own way.' We need to see, however, that there is only one acceptable way to praise God and that is the way he tells us to do it. 'Decency and order' does not mean we eliminate spontaneity, freedom or exuberance, but that we do something God's way. What many call 'decent' and 'orderly' is often indecent and disorderly as far as God is concerned. If you praise and worship 'your way', stop and start doing it God's way! Stubbornness, pride (what will others think?) half-heartedness and apathy are the main hindrances to true praise and worship.

However, it is not enough to praise because we are told to. What pleasure would that bring the Lord? Many Christians are like the stubborn little boy taken by his parents for dinner with their friends, who is told as they leave, 'Say thank you to the kind people.'

'I don't want to,' he replies.

'Say thank you,' the parent repeats, to no avail. This conversation continues, getting more heated, until eventually the irate parent whispers angrily, 'Say thank you, or else!'

(b) *For who God is*

Whatever may happen, God never changes. If we can find no other reason to praise and worship surely this is reason enough...he is worthy!

> Great and marvellous are your works, Lord God Almighty!
> Just and true are your ways,
> O King of the saints!
> Who shall not fear you, O Lord,
> And glorify your name?
> For you alone are holy.
> For all nations shall come and worship before you,
> For your judgments have been manifested
>
> (Rev 15:3–4)

> You are worthy, O Lord, to receive glory and honour and power: for you created all things, and by your will they exist and were created
>
> (Rev 4:11)

> Worthy is the Lamb who was slain to receive power and riches and wisdom and strength and honour and glory and blessing....
> Blessing and honour and glory and power be to him who sits on the throne, and to the Lamb, forever and ever
>
> (Rev 5:12–13).

In heaven, worship is not so much for what the Lord has done, but for who he is. He is worthy!

(c) *In gratitude for what he has done*

'Praise the Lord' has become a meaningless phrase to many Christians. We need to beware of taking the Lord's name in vain. When someone says 'Praise the Lord' I often ask them 'Why?' When David said, 'Praise the Lord', he usually gave a reason. 'Praise the Lord' is an exhortation rather than a statement.

'Praise him for his excellent greatness.'
'Praise him for his mighty deeds.'
'Praise the Lord; for the Lord is good.'

We have so much to praise him for. I have seen extremes in prayer, where people demand things of God, as if he were their loyal servant, rather than they his. Let us never get to the place where we take the Lord for granted, but praise him continually for his goodness to us!

> You have turned for me my mourning into dancing, you have put off my sackcloth and clothed me with gladness, to the end that my glory may sing praise to you and not be silent. O Lord my God, I will give thanks to you for ever (Ps 30:11–12).

(d) *Because it gets the Lord in true perspective*

Praise gets our eyes on the Lord. When we truly praise and worship we see him as he is. In David's psalms there are constant references to 'the Lord' and 'the King'. David had seen the King and the result of truly seeing him is praise and worship.

Praise de-centralizes self. It would be so easy when we consider that we are in God's army to get an inflated concept of our own importance. Jesus greeted his excited disciples, freshly returned from a 'successful ministry trip', eager to recount the miracles of healing and deliverances that had taken place, with the words, 'I give you the authority to trample on serpents and scorpions, and over all the power of the enemy, and nothing shall by any means hurt you. Nevertheless, do not rejoice in this, that the spirits are subject to you, but rejoice rather because your names are written in heaven' (Lk 10:19–20). It is true that the powers of darkness are subject to us in Christ's name. However, our real source of joy is that we are God's children, citizens of heaven. When being used by God is more important than our relationship with him, we are in a dangerous place. We must beware of becoming ministry or function centred, rather than God centred. Notice the order in which Jesus put things: 'You shall worship the Lord your God and him only you shall serve' (Mt 4:10). Worship comes before service. Our service must come out of a love relationship with the Lord.

He is not using us because he has to. God could finish everything off in a split second. He is Almighty. It is our privilege that he has chosen to use us. When I am complimented or hear a report of some tremendous miracle through my ministry, I seek later to get alone with God and thank him that it is he who has done it, and for the privilege of being used. It is the foolish things of this world God uses to confound the wise, the weak things of the world to put to shame the things which are mighty, so that no flesh can glory in his presence. No one can justifiably boast or get proud. Praise is a key to keeping things in the right perspective. There is no quicker way of losing your anointing and ministry than pride.

(e) *Because he is Lord*

Three weeks prior to leaving my employment and coming out into full-time ministry, I was driving home from Cornwall when my car began to skid. I shot across a grass verge, knocking down a sign (warning drivers to 'Take care, slippery roads') smashing a light and damaging the side of the car. Then the car fell down a short drop on to a verge, with one wheel completely over and the other on the edge of a ten foot drop. It all happened so quickly that all I had time to do was shout 'Jesus'. As I got out of the car and looked at the damage, the situation seemed disastrous with the crushed side, four flat tyres, the exhaust system torn off, a light smashed and the car covered in mud. It looked as though a bill for a few hundred pounds was coming my way and I had no idea where my next penny would come from! All I had was my savings of £40.

As I walked to the road side, planning to leave the car and hitchhike home, I gave the situation to God. Although I couldn't see how good could come out of it, I began to praise the Lord because he was in control, and Jesus was Lord of the situation. For a while no cars stopped. However, I had learned early in my ministry, when I had no car and hitch-hiked to minister, that the Lord has just the right car! I could confidently say, 'Thank you, Lord, that isn't good enough', as they sped past. Eventually a little mini stopped and I thanked the Lord for his choice. I explained to the driver what had happened as we walked over to view my car.

'If we could push it back, could you reverse it along the verge to the end and back up on to the road?' he asked.

I replied, 'You haven't seen my driving.'

He smiled and said, 'That's OK my friend in the car with me is a racing driver. I'll get him to do it.'

After his friend had neatly reversed the car back on to the road, I changed the worst tyre for my spare and drove home, a journey of over one hundred miles, still rather shaken up and thinking, 'I've had enough for one day, Lord, I'll drive home and buy new tyres tomorrow, they're ruined anyway.'

The next day I drove to the local garage to buy a new light and four new tyres. Knowing that the damage to the side of the car would cost well over £100, I decided to leave it and have it repaired later, when I could afford to. However, I was in for a few surprises. Firstly the attendant said, 'I've filled your tyres with air and none of them are damaged.'

'But I've just driven over one hundred miles with them like that,' I remarked, with surprise.

'Well, there's nothing wrong with those tyres.'

I asked him to fill up with petrol while I paid the £4 bill for the new light he had put on. As he was filling the tank the local car sprayer was viewing my car. When I walked back, he asked, 'Are you going to get that side repaired?'

I replied, 'I can't afford to at the moment.'

He thought for a minute and said, 'I'll do it in my spare time for you.' It cost me about £5…for a tip!

Next stop, the Exhaust Centre. As I drove in I noticed a large sign displaying their claim to stock every exhaust anyone could want. 'Oh, I'm sorry, sir, we have every exhaust…but yours,' came the embarrassed reply, 'but don't worry here are my vehicle's keys, borrow it for today, it's full of petrol. We'll get you the exhaust and fit it free at trade price.' The whole unit cost me £18.

The car was back on the road, as before, for less than £40. A miracle! Looking back, I think that did more for my faith than anything else. I wouldn't have missed it!

Being a Christian does not isolate us from difficulties. Believers are not immune to times of trouble, bereavement and pressure. Jesus did not try to deceive us but made it clear, 'In the world you have tribulation; but be of good cheer. I have overcome the world' (Jn 16:33). We can come out of any situation victorious. God has promised that he will turn anything Satan intends for harm, for our own good. He does not promise that all things will be 'good', but that all things will work together for good to them that love him (Rom 8:28). It is vital that we know this truth. If we don't, the situations we go through could throw us. We need to see that Jesus is on the throne! God knows what he is doing. Therefore, we can be of good cheer.

There have been many times when I have wondered, 'Lord, why are you letting this happen?' It has only been later, as I have looked back, that I could see the good that has come out of it. There have been some situations, though, that remain a mystery to me. I still don't know why God allowed them (maybe I'll have to wait till I get to heaven to find out) But I do trust him. He knows what he is doing—even if I have at times acknowledged this with tears in my eyes. He is Lord. He is King. He is on the throne!

Even when Paul and Silas were whipped and thrown into prison—at midnight they could praise the Lord. He turned it for good, with the jailor and all of his family being saved (Acts 16:25). They too ended up rejoicing (Acts 16:34)! Can you think of any circumstances less conducive to praise—beaten, imprisoned and at midnight? We are to be governed by our wills, submitting to the Lord and his word, not our emotions. That is why David could declare, 'I will bless the Lord at *all times*!' (Ps 34:1). He praised as an act of his will not just when he felt like it.

Satan wants us to think that God has lost control or has mistreated us. Yet even when we cannot fully understand why God should allow certain situations, we can praise God, realizing that he is still on the throne. He is big enough, powerful enough and loving enough to handle the situation. We can praise God 'at all times', 'continually' (Ps 34:1) and 'in everything' (1 Thess 5:18)!

Notice it is 'in all things' we are to give thanks, not 'for all things'. Jesus did not praise God for sickness, bondage or because Lazarus was dead. He rebuked the sickness and death and spoke life into the situation. Some would quote Ephesians 5:20 where we are exhorted to give thanks always for all things to God the Father in the name of our Lord Jesus Christ. However, the use of the word 'for' is an unfortunate translation. The Greek word is *Uper* meaning 'over', 'beyond' or 'above'. We are to praise over and above the situation, not for it. In spite of the situation, we can see over it, that Jesus is on the throne. Therefore we can praise. Remember Satan was not allowed to touch Job without God's permission (Job 1:10–12). God 'will not allow you to be tempted beyond what you are able' to stand (1 Cor 10:13). At times it may appear that way, because we are just being stretched a little more than last time! He is on the throne! God doesn't make mistakes!

In recent days many have testified that God has allowed the pressure to be increased in their lives. He wants a people who will stand firm and obey his every command, who will not run when things get tough.

Why is it that Christians get angry, frustrated and impatient? It happens when we lose sight of the fact that 'all things work together for good to those who love God, to those who are called according to his purpose' (Rom 8:28), that he is on the throne. We can miss God's best through disobedience, but when I am walking in obedience to him, nothing can go wrong!

(f) *A mighty weapon*

I believe that praise is one of our mightiest weapons against our enemy. Praise is practical. When Israel began to praise the Lord, he went to work on their behalf. 2 Chronicles chapter 20 records how, in response to his people's praise, the Lord set an ambush against the armies of Ammon, Moab and Mount Seir who had declared war on Israel. There is power in praise. Satan is allergic to praise for God inhabits the praises of his people (see Ps 22:3). When God's people truly praise him, his presence is manifest. The presence of God always expels Satan.

Praise also sets us free from 'religiosity'. It is usually the 'religious' Christians who refuse to praise God the way he commands. I have seen some outstanding releases in people's lives when they have begun to praise (even if they didn't 'feel' like it when they started).

(g) *It is a testimony to the world*

Praise is one of the greatest tools in evangelism. Psalm 40:3 tells us 'he has put a new song in my mouth—praise to our God; many will see it and fear, and will trust in the Lord.' God inhabits the praises of his people and when we praise him, those around are made aware of his presence and reality, and their need of him. True praise and worship softens and prepares hearts, builds faith and makes us sensitive to the Holy Spirit as nothing else can.

Often in our local church and also during crusades around the country, we will go out into the streets (sometimes two hundred or more of us) and praise and worship the Lord, interspersing our songs and praise with positive testimonies and drama. If the people won't come to us, we'll go to them and many are saved out on the streets.

The world needs to see the reality of Christ. There is more 'praise' at football matches than most church meetings. Let us not forget that Pentecost began with praising not preaching. Their praise, however, raised questions: 'Why are those ordinary people so excited and enjoying themselves?' That made a grand opening for Peter to preach the gospel.

(h) *It unites us*

One of my observations at charismatic rallies is how brethren from many different backgrounds are united as they praise and worship. Baptists, Methodists, Anglicans, Pentecostals and Catholics, to name a few, standing, kneeling, hands raised, worship their Lord and King. True praise and worship transforms us from a congregation to a family. It demonstrates openly who is the centre of our lives.

In 2 Chronicles 5:13–14 we read that when the Ark was brought into the temple 'the trumpeters and singers were *as one* to make one sound to be heard in praising and thanking the Lord, and when they lifted up their voice with the trumpets and cymbals and instruments of music, and praised the Lord saying, "For he is good, for his mercy endures forever" that the house, the house of the Lord was filled with a cloud, so that the priests could not continue ministering because of the cloud; for the glory of the Lord filled the house.'

How we today need to see the Ark (a sign of God's lordship and presence) returned to the temple (the church being the temple of the Holy Spirit).

Praise the Lord!
Praise God in his sanctuary;
Praise him in his mighty firmament!
Praise him for his mighty acts;
Praise him according to his excellent greatness!
Praise him with the sound of the trumpet;
Praise him with the lute and harp!
Praise him with the timbrel and dance;

Praise him with stringed instruments and flutes!
Praise him with loud cymbals;
Praise him with high sounding cymbals!
Let everything that has breath praise the Lord.
Praise the Lord!

(Ps 150)

12

United We Stand

We have considered one major problem: the lack of wrestling against 'principalities' and 'powers'. The second major problem is that much of our fighting is against the wrong things. Paul wrote—'We do not wrestle against flesh and blood' (Eph 6:12). However, so often Christians fight against other people, usually other Christians. We are called to spiritual warfare against the powers of darkness, not to carnal warfare against each other. So often Christians turn and begin wrestling with their own partner while the enemy stands by watching and laughing as we do his work for him.

Are you a cannibal?

The Bible talks of those who 'bite and devour one another' (Gal 5:15). Much of what is called 'sharing' is really no more than gossiping. 'You must pray for brother so and so, he's really having a hard time….' Does such sharing come from a heart of love? Does it 'edify' the hearer? Or is it shared maliciously to reveal another brother's weakness? Does it grieve the Holy Spirit (Eph 4:29–30)? Paul said, 'If one member suffers, all the members suffer with it' and, 'If one member is honoured, all the members rejoice with it' (1 Cor 12:26). This is how it should be. Yet, far too often this scripture could be written, 'When one member suffers, all the members criticize him, when one member is honoured, all the members get jealous!' Such carnal behaviour needs to be dealt with before God can use us to fight against our true enemy. Criticism is no less than shooting down a fellow soldier.

When Saul met with Jesus on the Damascus road, Jesus confronted him with a stunning question, 'Saul, Saul, why are you persecuting me?' (Acts 9:4). Notice the words of the question were not, 'Why are you persecuting my church?' but, 'Why are you persecuting me?' Jesus had already ascended back to heaven. How could Saul persecute him? The Lord takes the treatment of his church personally! How we treat our fellow Christian is how we treat Jesus.

'If someone says, "I love God," and hates his brother, he is a liar' (1 Jn 4:20). Yet often Christians are the most judgemental, backbiting and suspicious people around. They are critical about other Christians, other leaders, other churches. Do we believe we will see a mighty move of God with such sin openly practised and overlooked in the church? Do you persecute Jesus? Many church buildings have two doorways, which conveniently means Christians who do not get on with others can leave without having to meet. Pastors frequently comment on members: 'They are such good Christians, they attend all the meetings, pay their tithes, they don't smoke and agree with all the church doctrines.' Yet often these same saints are notorious gossips! This is very serious. The Scriptures make it very clear, 'Whoever hates his brother is a murderer, and you know that no murderer has eternal life abiding in him' (1 Jn 3:15). Do we really believe that scripture?

Be reconciled

It is time to quit our petty squabbling. There is much truth in the old saying, 'United we stand, divided we fall'.

On a number of occasions I have had to seek out brethren so that I may be reconciled with them, often to say I was sorry for some way in which I had hurt them. Some of the brothers I am closest to today are those who I have had to go and be reconciled with and on a number of occasions we have ended up in tears in each other's arms. Peter asked Jesus, 'How often shall my brother sin against me, and I forgive him? Up to seven times?' (How generous.)

Jesus replied, 'I do not say to you, up to seven times, but up to seventy times seven' (Mt 18:21–22). There may well have been those who have sinned against you. You may say 'They don't deserve to be forgiven.' However, Jesus warns us, 'If you do not forgive men their trespasses, neither will your Father forgive your trespasses' (Mt 6:14–15). To pray, 'Forgive us our debts, as we forgive our debtors' (Mt 6:12), is another way of praying, 'Lord if I won't forgive those who have sinned against me, do not forgive me.' We are to forgive as he has forgiven us—totally, and unreservedly. That's quite a prayer.

Our wrestling is not against flesh and blood. The things that really hurt are often done by those who do not want to hurt us and usually do not realize what they have done. Jesus prayed, 'Father forgive them for they do not know what they do' (Lk 23:34). When we feel used, we have an opportunity to be kind to the 'unthankful and evil' (Lk 6:35). For, 'If you love those who love you, what credit is that to you? For even sinners love those who love them' (Lk 6:32). Jesus brought a stern warning, 'Judge not, and you shall not be judged. Condemn not, and you shall not be condemned. Forgive, and you will be forgiven' (Lk 6:37). Many Christians live with bitterness and resentment against others who have hurt, overlooked, rejected, slandered and mistreated them. The reaction may appear justified but when we review another's sin against us in the light of how much God has forgiven us, there is no excuse. We are called to forgive and forget, refusing to bring up the subject again. Praying for God's blessing on the offenders and seeking to serve them, can dramatically change your attitude towards them. 'Love your enemies, bless those who curse you, do good to those who hate you, and pray for those who spitefully use you and persecute you' (Mt 5:44).

It would be good to take a few moments to review your relationship with others. Is there someone you resent or hold a grudge against, someone you need to forgive and be reconciled with?

The Scriptures are clear, 'If you bring your gift to the altar, and there remember that your brother has something against you, leave your gift there before the altar, and go your way. First be reconciled to your brother, and then come and offer your gift' (Mt 5:23–24). What will you do about it?

Let us endeavour 'to keep the unity of the Spirit in the bond of peace' (Eph 4:3). Unity is not something we have to produce, it is something we already have in Christ. Our call is to endeavour to keep it. It is so easy to allow a misunderstanding or a minor problem to be magnified, and unless we endeavour to keep the unity (which requires working at) a rift so easily takes place. If such a rift has been allowed to happen, the longer it is left without seeking reconciliation, the further apart we drift. Now that the wall of division has been broken down between us and God, he wants to break down the walls that divide us from one another.

Amen

There is something powerful in saints being united. In Matthew 18:19 Jesus promised, 'If two of you agree on earth concerning anything that they ask, it will be done for them by my Father in heaven. For where two or three are gathered together in my name, I am there in the midst of them.' I remember as a new Christian attending prayer meetings and spending the first half hour plucking up courage to pray. Just as I went to pray someone else would come out with the exact prayer that I was about to bring, causing me to go home disappointed that someone else had 'stolen my prayer'. What I did not realize was how exciting that is. It means we have 'agreed' in prayer and in such an event Jesus has promised, 'It shall be done for them by my Father in heaven.' Amen means 'So be it'. When I say 'Amen' to another prayer I am saying, 'Lord, I agree, so be it.' A husband and wife who agree in prayer are one of the mightiest forces on earth.

(a) *Unity in our families*

Jesus wants to, 'Turn the hearts of the fathers to the children and the hearts of the children to their fathers' (Mal 4:6). He wants to reunite families. When a couple will come unreservedly to God, who is the source of love, he can put love back where it has been lost. With so many pressures and 'important' things to do, it is all too easy to neglect our families. Yet such neglect has adverse consequences. We need to be right with one another. In a society where family life is breaking up there is probably no greater witness for the Lord than a family who are living for the Lord and are not afraid to demonstrate their love for one another. The family typifies the 'two or three' who can agree on earth and see their requests granted. We will miss so much if we do not pray together as families.

God has ordained roles for each member of the family. Any deviance from that role will aid disunity. We need to discover our role and fit in (see Eph 5:22 – 6:4). In that way we can enjoy unity and peace. God's way works!

(b) *Racial harmony*

Our lands are fast becoming multi-racial communities but there is a pervading attitude of racial superiority among many. For the Christian, however, there is no excuse for colour prejudice. 'He who hates his brother is in darkness' (1 Jn 2:11). 'Brotherhood' is the result of sonship. We have the same Father. It is 'upon all flesh' that God is pouring out his Spirit (Acts 2:17). By his blood Christ has purchased *one people, one nation* from 'Every tribe and tongue'. We are nationals of heaven. We are not really British, our true citizenship is not on earth but in heaven. In reality we are not 'multi-racial' but one new race, where no man is 'known after the flesh' (whether it be black, red, yellow, brown, green or white). We need to be uncoloured in our thinking—brethren from all backgrounds, dwelling together in unity! This is not a call for losing our cultural traditions. As long as they are godly, they can add spice to life. The 'Judaisers' were condemned in the early church for insisting that Gentile converts adopt the Jewish culture and practice. God even had to give the apostle Peter a vision to overcome his racial prejudices (Acts 10). It is now time for the church to rise up and proclaim to our world of conflict and confusion the divine solution to racial disharmony.

(c) *Unity in the local church*

Unity in the local church needs to begin among the leadership. If they are divided, the people will be divided also, but a united leadership can work together towards a united church. I am encouraged that Paul could write to the disunited and divided church at Corinth, 'Now I plead with you, brethren, by the name of our Lord Jesus Christ, that you all *speak the same thing*, and that there will be *no divisions* among you, but that you be *perfectly joined together* in the *same mind and* in the *same judgement*' (1 Cor 1:10). If that was possible at Corinth, surely it is possible for us.

(d) *You in your small corner*

It is so easy, too, to become exclusive and write off other Christians and local churches because they are not part of our group. Like the disciples of old, we come to the Lord and say, 'Master, we saw someone casting out demons in your name, and we forbade him because he does not follow with us.' Have you noticed that the Lord was not impressed but said, 'Do not forbid him, for he who is not against us is for us' (Lk 9:49–50)? We are a 'holy nation' (1 Pet 2.9) not a holy 'denomination'.

I have firmly sought to abide by God's command not to touch his anointed (1 Chron 16:22). If God is anointing a ministry, I dare not be critical of it. God is the great Judge, not me. Yet it is so easy to set ourselves up as judge and jury.

Even when King Saul was out of fellowship and in disobedience to God, David did not try to overthrow or slander him, but treated him with respect, refusing to kill him even when the opportunity arose.

I believe it is possible to be of different tribes, like Israel of old, yet one nation. We need to realize that variety is not the enemy of unity. A look at the world in which we live demonstrates this fact. The snow flakes on the ground are unique, not one blade of grass is the same as another, and you and I are all different! Most Christians want unity, as long as everyone else believes exactly what they believe! The possibility this side of heaven of our agreeing on every point is outside the realm of my faith. I do not believe that God is calling for unity at the cost of compromising vital truth. The Bible talks of 'streams in the desert' (Is 35:6). The streams come out of one river source and are wholesome. Each stream reaches different people, those which the others couldn't reach. The unifying factor is that our life source is the same river! I am not teaching that denominational and doctrinal differences are God's intention but we need to stop being bigoted and recognize that God is moving among others from different groups to our own. If he will fellowship with them, can we write them off? Are we a higher authority? Someone has re-written the well-known hymn, 'Like a mighty army moves the church of God', to read, 'Like a mighty tortoise moves the church of God, brothers we are treading where we've always trod. We are all divided, many bodies we, very strong on doctrine weak on charity'.

It is time to start fighting against our common enemy instead of one another. As long as we continue to be full of grudges and exclusive, the church will remain unnoticed. However, a church demonstrating God's divine love will make an impact on our land. A statement which has challenged me is, 'I want no fewer brothers than God has sons.' Do you? I believe that it saddens God's heart when there are churches in the same locality each desiring to see the kingdom of God extended yet unwilling to have fellowship together because of minor disagreements. I believe God calls for a reconciliation. The practicalities of this will have to be worked out from area to area, but where there is vision and a will, there is a way.

Jesus prayed for his followers that they, 'may be one, as

you, Father, are in me, and I in you; that they also may be one in us, that the world may believe that you sent me' (Jn 17:21). Unity is a vital key to effectiveness in evangelism.

'Behold how good and how pleasant it is for brethren to dwell together in unity!...For *there the Lord commanded the blessing*—life for evermore' (Ps 133:1, 3).

Not against flesh and blood

When I was in secular employment I remember working alongside a woman who at that time did not like me and deliberately sought to annoy me. My first reaction was one of frustration. My second reaction was one of anger, mingled with a desire for revenge. One day, as I was even contemplating giving up my job because of her, I was reading through the word of God and came across Ephesians 6:12. It hit me that I had been wrestling against flesh and blood when I had been called to wrestle against principalities and powers. I began to see that principalities and powers were influencing this woman although she was unaware of it. I began to rebuke and command them to loose her and found that almost immediately her attitude towards me changed and before I left the job we were friends. I am not implying that in prayer we have authority over other people's wills. Even almighty God is a perfect Gentleman and has given man free-will. He will not force us to act against our will. However, we can pray against the powers of darkness that *blind* people's spiritual eyes and *bind* them from seeing the truth and turning to the Lord.

If only the time spent moaning about the ungodliness in our land could be devoted to dealing with our invisible enemy who seeks to destroy our land!

God gave the promised land to his people Israel and commanded them to possess it. They had to realize that the land belonged to God and the people who were then living in it were squatters. God had given his people the right to forcefully evict any squatters they encountered on their journey. Israel's journey to the land of promise should have lasted eleven days; however, forty years later they still had not arrived (Deut 1:2). Forty years had been spent in the wilderness in unbelief, discontent, criticism of the Lord, Moses and his leadership, and the longing to return to Egypt. Because of their disobedience God let that whole generation pass away so that he could start again with a new people. Let this be a warning to us. Let us quit fighting against God, and one another and rise up to be the army God has called us to be, lest we too miss out on what God has planned for us.

13

We're In It Together

We often hear it said that you don't have to go to church to be a Christian. Is that true? The statement is usually made as a result of a misunderstanding of what 'church' really is. The word church (Greek *ekklesia*) means 'a called out people', called out of the world and called together. We are the church! The church is made up of people, not buildings. A building can *never* be a church. At the most it is a building where the church meets. I get concerned when people say to me, 'We are painting the church this week.' (I visualize Christians being lined up and smothered in paint!) We are the church; twenty-four hours a day, seven days a week. When I meet with another Christian, that is a church meeting! The *universal church* is made up of every single Christian (whatever tag they may or may not wear). The church is made up of 'living stones' being 'built up' as 'a spiritual house' (1 Pet 2:5) not lifeless bricks! We are the 'house of God', the temple of the Holy Spirit, not a bricks and mortar building (1 Cor 6:19). Christians do not 'go to' church; they are church!

However, it is not enough to be part of the universal church, every Christian should be committed to a *local church*.

Most of the New Testament was written to local churches and loses its meaning when taken out of that context. There is one army (universal church), but many corps (local churches) and it is God who does the posting. He has 'set the members, *each one of them*, in the body just as he pleased' (1 Cor 12:18). Every Christian belongs somewhere! No one is called to be a Kamikaze pilot. Independent soldiers, going their own way and doing their own thing, are of no real value to God's army. Commitment to a local corp is vital! However, let us make sure that we are in the right place, as commitment can be bad, if we are committed to something God is not committed to!

The world can dismiss a single Christian as 'strange' but a group of believers, differing in temperament and background, yet committed to God and one another cannot easily be ignored. We are called to demonstrate the life of God in our locality. The old evangelical adage, 'Don't look at the church, look at Jesus' is both unscriptural and a 'cop out' too. We are 'the body of Christ' (1 Cor 12:27), Jesus' physical manifestation on earth. We are God's representatives to this world!

The local church should be somewhere where we receive:

(a) *Comradeship*

Church, first and foremost, is family. Yet many local churches are more like 'self-service restaurants', where a person can go to get food, without having to make contact with other people. The world's comment on the early church was 'see how they love one another'. All of us need to know that we are loved and wanted. We need to know that there are those we can freely go to at any time. All of us need encouragement and often honest confrontation. We are called to 'bear one another's burdens' (Gal 6:2). That is costly and a major reason why so much of church life is superficial and unreal. Shallow relationships are a recipe for loneliness. Church also involves caring for each other, materially and practically (Acts 2:40–47; 4:32–37) and that certainly is costly! It is far more than the weekly handshake and 'wasn't that a lovely message. See you next Sunday?' How worldly! Even non-Christian clubs share more fellowship than that! The Greek word for fellowship (*koinonia*) was the word used to describe business partners who had agreed to share their assets, and a husband and wife who had committed themselves to sharing their lives!

Church is not primarily meetings. Often when Christians say, 'We have fellowship meetings twice a week', they really mean, 'We sit for an hour looking at the back of someone's head, twice a week.' What fellowship is that? What do we find out about each other? (Whether the person in front has dandruff?) How do we get to know each other this way? Meetings are vital, but church is primarily what takes place outside meetings; it is a daily building of our lives together. If we are going to truly fellowship, we may need to reconsider our weekly programmes. Many local churches have so many meetings, that there is no time left for fellowship or family life! Some are proud of the fact that they have something on every day of the week!

(b) *Food*

Spiritually undernourished soldiers will lack strength to fight, be inefficient and soon die (1 Pet 2:2; Col 1:28). For this reason, numerous starved Christians have moved on to greener pastures. The accusation of 'sheep stealing' has been made of many leaders in recent years. However, usually a far more accurate statement would be that they grow grass! We must allow people to settle where they will flourish. Who wants a congregation of people whose hearts are not in the work? Surely it is much better that they join a local church to which they can really commit themselves.

(c) *Development of gifts*

The church should be the one real place in society where there is no class, age or racial discrimination; a people drawn from all walks of life, yet united by a common love for Jesus. We are all different and therefore we complement one another. God has not made us carbon copies of each other. 'The body is not one member but many' (1 Cor 12:14). Therefore, 'The eye cannot say to the hand, "I have no need of you"; nor again the head to the feet, "I have no need of you." No, much rather those members of the body which seem to be weaker are necessary' (1 Cor 12:21–22). We need one another! You might not be a part of intelligence, paratroops, tanks or SAS…but *you* have a vital part to play! In an earthly army, ordering the food supplies may not bring you national acclaim! You might not be regarded as a hero or receive a Victoria Cross! Yet the mundane jobs are vital. The soldiers out front will have little effect if the storeman forgets to resupply! We need each other! 'There are diversities of gifts, but the same Spirit. There are differences of ministries, but the same Lord…The manifestation of the Spirit is given to each one for the profit of all' (1 Cor 12:4–7).

(d) *Training*

To go to battle without proper training would be suicidal. It is useless to have all the weapons we need (as we have) if we do not know how to use them and how to recognize our enemy and his tactics. What is more, we all need to be helped in our weaknesses and to have our good points developed. The local church should include teaching to the church as a whole and also one-to-one teaching.

Jesus spent his prime time training a few men to take over when he left them. He did not spend his time trying to sort out those who did not want to be 'sorted out', but with those who really meant business. He lived, walked, talked and performed his miracles with them around. He shared his whole life with them. They were his disciples, or, to use modern terms, his apprentices. He then sent them off saying, 'Go, therefore and make disciples (apprentices) of all nations' (Mt 28:19). They would have known no other way of doing it, than the way Jesus had done it! When my brother Ian decided that he wanted to be a carpenter, he sought a skilled man and became his apprentice. Now, himself a skilled carpenter, he can train others. Jesus put it this way, 'A disciple is not above his teacher, but everyone who is perfectly trained will be *like* his teacher' (Lk 6:40). Success without a successor is failure.

Paul said to Timothy (a man he had trained) 'My son, be

strong in the grace that is in Christ Jesus. And the things that you have heard from me among many witnesses, commit these to *faithful men* who will be able to teach others also' (2 Tim 2:1–2). He exhorted the older women to 'admonish the young women to love their husbands, to love their children, to be discreet, chaste, homemakers, good, obedient to their own husbands, that the word of God may not be blasphemed' (Tit 2:3–5).

(e) *Leadership*

After people have been evangelized they need to be pastorized!! Trial and error is not the best way to learn! Every Christian needs to be cared for. Therefore when a church is too large for one man to adequately care for its members a pastoral team will be needed. Such teams have led to amazing growth in churches around the world.

As the Lord looked out over the multitude, he saw a people who were 'weary and scattered like sheep having no shepherd' (Mt 9:36–38). A shepherd should provide food, protection, care and direction for his sheep, but, without true shepherds, the people were scattered and fainted. They were 'distressed and downcast'. The word distressed actually means 'torn and mangled'. A sheep who has no shepherd is prey to all kinds of accidents and attacks by wild beasts (cf Ezek 34:8). A lot of my ministry in the past has been counselling people who are 'torn and mangled' because they are sheep without a shepherd!

It is interesting to note that it was in the context of 'sheep without shepherds' that Jesus spoke of the labourers being few and exhorts us to therefore pray for their raising up! Proper maintenance is far better than emergency jobs! Many of the so-called 'best churches', are no more than preaching centres. One might as well stay at home as to go to them for fellowship and care. An army is not made up of individuals doing their own thing! God's army is made up of people built together, and submitted to the leadership that he has appointed. The Lord raises up leaders to bring his direction to the corp, men who can recognize his voice and will faithfully and fearlessly move with him. How we need leaders empowered by the Holy Spirit with wisdom, maturity and godly lives (1 Tim 3: 1–7; Tit 1:5–9)!

Any talk about 'leadership' causes fear in many. Stories of abuse and misuse of authority are not too hard to find. However, let us not throw out the baby with the bath water. Submission and obedience might not be popular words to many but the Scriptures clearly teach the submission and obedience of children to parents, wives to husbands, slaves to masters and the church to its leaders (Eph 5:22; 6:9). No leader is infallible. However, a leader who, like the Lord, is teachable and approachable and is himself submissive and seeking his people's highest good, is not hard to submit to. Jesus made it clear that leaders must not lord it, as worldly leaders and dictators do, but lead primarily by example (Mt 20:25–28).

The teaching, 'I obey no man, only God' is unscriptural and usually a pseudo spiritual cover-up for rebellion. The Scriptures tell us, 'obey those who rule over you, and be submissive, for they watch out for your souls, as those who must give account' (Heb 13:7, 17). To say to the major, 'I'll only do what the king tells me', is ridiculous. The king has delegated his authority to the major. In obeying the major you are obeying the king.

God's method of rule is not democracy, where the soldiers take a vote on the way ahead, but, theocracy, where he tells the leaders which way to go and then they declare, 'This is the way we believe God wants us to go, who's coming?' If Moses had taken a vote on whether Israel worshipped the Lord or the golden calf, it would have been around four and a half million to one, including the assistant pastor, Aaron! The leader who continues to be pulled in all directions by factions in his congregation, and is constantly seeking to please everyone, signs a contract for a nervous breakdown, and sooner or later (usually sooner) a split church.

How we need to hear God telling us afresh which way to go. The fact that a certain method worked once is no guarantee that it will always work. Many a church structure has become an 'old wineskin' (Lk 5:33–39): hard, rigid and unresponsive to the Holy Spirit. So, as God has been pouring out. the new wine of the Holy Spirit, the inevitable has happened. Just as Jesus said it would, splits have occurred. God will not compromise. You cannot put new wine into old wineskins. A leader who moves with God will not be popular with those who do not want to. And when leaders will not move with God they must be prepared to lose those who do want to. If they won't move with him, he'll soon find someone else who will.

Tozer put it this way, 'Unless we intend to reform, we may as well not pray.' Moving with God is costly. We must be flexible in God's hands.

(f) *Taking ground*

As we have considered the vital place of the local church in the believer's life, let us not forget our primary calling. Many local churches have become so exclusive that they are like monastic communities! We are not here to entertain saints. It is time to stop playing at church. We have a call and should be seeing growth both in maturity and in numbers. Our love for one another, the holiness of our lives and the signs and wonders God is doing in our midst should be beginning to affect our area.

True biblical evangelism must be grounded in the local church. Christians in a locality who are all out for God and properly relating to one another are the greatest possible threat to Satan's kingdom: there is nothing he hates more.

14

Charge!

I was challenged recently by a little cartoon picturing a busy High Street at Christmas time with shoppers milling around laden with Christmas trees, presents and tinsel. From one side of the street to the other hung a banner reading 'Glory to God in the Highest'. However, the 'e' had fallen out from the 'Highest' and lay on the pavement, so that the banner read 'Glory to God in the High st'! Below, as two young lads stood looking up at it, one said to the other, 'Perhaps that's how God meant it to be.'

It is time for God's glory to be seen in the High Street!

In the book of Acts most of the miracles and sharing of the gospel took place where they could be seen…out on the streets. For too long we have 'hidden' the demonstrations of the gospel in our buildings. For too long most of the life in the Spirit has been reserved for mid-week meetings in homes, lest it offends others who do not want to move with God, while the basic life and attitude of the church remains unaffected. I believe that this hiding the gospel is a major cause of the apparent ineffectiveness in evangelism up until now. The Book of Acts tells us, 'This thing was not done in a corner' (Acts 26:26). Could we say that? We put up our signs. We proclaim, 'Come to us, you're welcome to join us any time you wish'. Ignoring Jesus' words that the world is blind, deaf and lost. What use are such signs to the blind? Very few will come to Christ this way. Our call is to go and get them, to go out into the streets, lanes, highways and hedges and 'compel them to come in' (Lk 14:21–23). When did you last do that? It is time to take the kingdom!

Retreat or advance?

Though I would not deny that God has been shaping up his church for the task ahead, I believe that for too long we have been introverted. We have a commission. We may not feel ready. But were the Christians in the Book of Acts ready? After his resurrection Jesus appeared to his fearful, hiding disciples and in one breath he rebuked them for their unbelief, while with the next he commissioned them to preach the gospel to the whole world, healing the sick and casting out demons (Mk 16:14–18). Days later three thousand were added to the church. Were they ready? The church has been sent into enemy-held territory to take ground. Yet it is so easy to retreat into the security of our cosy fellowships, ignoring what is going on in the nasty world around us. It is so easy to shut ourselves in our 'upper rooms' while our world falls headlong into hell.

How we need to recapture the zeal the early Christians had which drove them out into their world. They realized that each person won for Jesus is someone claimed from Satan's kingdom.

Readjusted priorities

Apart from worship, evangelizing is the church's foremost responsibility. Before the consummation of the kingdom, 'the gospel must first be preached to all nations' (Mk 13:10). Now we have been reconciled, we have been given the ministry of reconciliation. It is so easy to become introverted and neglect this responsibility. For too long 'evangelism' has been left to the 'experts'. It's no excuse to say, 'I'm not an evangelist' or 'That's what we have a pastor for'. Neither can we say, 'I'll go if God calls me.' Jesus' words are clear. 'Go into all the world and preach the gospel to every creature' (Mk 16:15). You have the call! Physically we might not be able to reach all the lost in the world, but we can share with those around us and by prayer and giving take the gospel to the whole world. While there are still unsaved, you have the call! The early church did not wait for a specific call. Where they saw need, they went, unless God closed the door (Acts 16:6–19). Someone put it this way, 'It is the sheep that have the lambs, not the shepherds' and 'healthy sheep have lambs'. Although some Christians are especially gifted to be evangelists that does not excuse others from sharing their faith. Every Christian is called to 'do the work of an evangelist' (2 Tim 4:5). No one can say it is not his ministry!

In Scripture the evangelist's major function is to equip the saints for the work of the ministry, to teach them to evangelize (Eph 4:11, 12). God's desire is not just for evangelists but for an evangelistic people!

To the early Christians nothing was more natural than sharing the good news of what Jesus had done for them and demonstrating it by their lives together. The authorities sought to silence them by persecution. However, as they were scattered they 'went everywhere preaching the word'. Major public rallies played a part in their evangelism (Acts 2:14; 3:11; 8:5–6; 17:22). But it seems that the major means of spreading the gospel was the daily witness of all the Christians.

'Call in the witness'

'You shall receive power when the Holy Spirit has come upon you; and you shall be witnesses to me in Jerusalem, and in all Judea and Samaria, and to the end of the earth' (Acts 1:8). The word witness means to give or to provide evidence for that which we have seen and heard and know: to provide proof. The gospel of the kingdom can be both seen and heard. Individually and corporately we are to be witnesses by our whole life and lifestyle. We are not just to *give* evidence but to *be* evidence. Often it is only a consistent godly lifestyle that opens the way for us to talk effectively about the Lord. The man in the street will judge Christianity by what he sees in us. The Christian soldier is always on duty. The world will watch you on Monday morning. They will watch how you keep your promises, how you treat your parents, how you behave at school, how you work, how you react in a crisis. Our lives should provoke questions like, 'Why are you different/so happy/so caring?' 'What have you got that I haven't?' This offers a natural opening to sharing what the Lord has done. After Jesus had set the Gadarene demoniac free, he told him, 'Return to your own house, and tell what great things God has done for you' (Lk 8:39). That is being a witness. You might not be called to be a witness to the 'ends of the earth' but you are called to be a witness in your 'Jerusalem', that is, where you are now.

Paul exhorts the wives of unbelievers to so demonstrate kingdom life that 'without a word' their husbands may be won by their conduct (1 Pet 3:1–2). Our sharing of the gospel is not so much words as lifestyle. This in turn should lead to opportunities to share verbally too. We should seek to be the best husband, wife, parent, child, brother or sister and love, care for, serve and befriend those close to us. We are to have our 'conduct honourable among the Gentiles, that when they speak against you as evil-doers, they may, by your good works which they observe, glorify God in the day of visitation' (1 Pet 2:12). Even if there seems to be little fruit at the moment from your witness, be patient, don't give up. I believe our land is in for a mighty visitation of God and then much of the seed sown in the past will be reaped! You may have made mistakes in the past, but don't let that hinder you now. God can turn an apparently hopeless situation to good.

To be a 'witness' has legal connotations. If you see a crime committed, your qualification to be a 'witness' is not a great ability to speak, or a dynamic personality. Your qualification is that you were there and can bring first hand evidence. In a court of law it is of little value to say, 'My friend told me about the crime he saw committed.' The court only wants to hear first hand experience: 'I witnessed this myself.' When told by the authorities to stop sharing about Jesus, Peter and John replied, 'We cannot but speak of the things which we have seen and heard' (Acts 4:20). If the gospel is important to you, you'll want to share it!

You may not regard your testimony as 'dynamic'. However, it is special and unique. (By saying 'your testimony' I am not referring to just what God did, but, what he is doing now.) Some find it helpful to write parts of their testimony out, not to read to others, but to help clarify in their own mind how they met with Jesus and what differences he has made. It also helps prune the religious terminology which would be a foreign language to the unsaved. Be real. Other people are now facing many of the situations you have been through; but they are without Jesus. Our world is full of bound, lonely, hurt, fearful and depressed people, struggling under mental pressure to find a reason to live. Behind the doors of many respectable homes families are breaking up. Many 'religious' people are striving futilely to earn their way to heaven. Yet most have never heard the gospel, even once! What most unsaved people conceive a Christian to be, is far removed from the truth. Man was made for a relationship with God and instinctively seeks for him. Our world is seeking for Jesus, even if it does not realize it. There can be no real lasting fulfilment in life outside a relationship with him. We are called to 'shine as lights in the world' (Phil 2:15), to stand out in our darkened world.

David Watson in his book, *I Believe in Evangelism* (published by Hodder & Stoughton) puts it this way:

> I have learned that most people, if not all, are basically hungry for God even when they show little sign of this on the surface. Jesus knew what was in man. Outward appearances are notoriously deceptive, and the heart of man will always be empty until filled with the one Person for whom he was created. A man may deny that food exists but he will still be physically hungry for he is made that way, and a man may deny that God exists, but he will be spiritually hungry, for he is made that way. 'I tell you,' said Jesus to his disciples, 'lift up your eyes and see how the fields are already white for harvest' (John 4:35, RSV). Most people are

much more ready for God, or much nearer God, than we might imagine.

You don't have to look far, the harvest is ripe, waiting to be reaped. Yet many Christians hesitate to share their faith for fear that others might ask them questions they are unable to answer. There is no need to be ashamed to say, 'I don't know, but I'll try to find out the answer for you' and then to study God's word on the subject and seek someone who can help you. You are called to 'be ready to give a defence to everyone who asks you a reason for the hope that is in you' (1 Pet 3:15). The early Christians were not great learned men, but 'uneducated and untrained men'. The Greek puts it *agrammatoi idiotai*, literally 'ungrammatical idiots'. However, the evidence that they had been with Jesus was indisputable—the disciples' lives were changed and the man lame for over forty years stood before them totally healed. I was thrilled when I heard Billy Graham share how the actor Steve McQueen had become a Christian before he died. One of the things though, that blessed me the most, was that it wasn't Billy who led him to the Lord, but some unknown plane instructor who was giving Steve flying lessons.

Have you noticed that some of the greatest sermons in the Bible were to individuals? Think of Jesus' discourse with Nicodemus (John 3) and the woman at the well (John 4), Paul before Felix the governor (Acts 24) and Philip with the Ethiopian Chancellor of the Exchequer (Acts 8). We are told that hundreds of years later when missionaries went to Ethiopia, the country had already been evangelized—the result of one dignitary being led to the Lord!

Missionaries wanted

A doctor working in this country is called a GP, but if he goes to do the same work abroad we call him a missionary. Is this reasonable? We need missionaries as much as any country! I believe that God has called every Christian to be a missionary. You rub shoulders with those no one else could reach.

Maybe your call is 'Mission to the school/college or teachers'; 'Mission to your neighbours or family'; 'Mission to the office or factory'; 'Mission to the dustman or milkman'; 'Mission to your husband, wife or parents'. After I left 'Mission to the school', I went to work for a while as a 'Missionary to the National Westminster Bank' before the world became my parish. Remember, it is only after we have been witnesses in Jerusalem that we qualify to go to Judea, Samaria and the ends of the earth. With God, there is no 'secular employment'. Every Christian is in full time missionary service! A vocation is not something limited to preachers, neither is the kingdom of God just for Sundays!

We are called to stand out in our places of employment because of our attitudes to our employers, workmates, subordinates and customers. Because we are not late for work, because of our wholeheartedness at work in a day of casualness, because of our impeccable honesty and justice in transactions people take note of us. Our testimony is primarily visual, and should lead to opportunities to talk about the Lord with colleagues. This is usually far more effective than standing on the table in the canteen pronouncing impending doom on your feasting fellow workers.

You are called to 'let your light so shine before men, that they may see your good works and glorify your Father in heaven' (Mt 5:16).

We need missionaries!

Britain can no longer be called a Christian country. Our legal, social and educational standards have moved far from the standards set in God's word. Many have roots in the theories of men like Freud (who called himself a 'hopeless pagan') and Darwin. Not too many years ago there were areas of right and wrong which you could identify. Now there is no standard to check and dictate behaviour: 'If it feels good, do it'. We are now reaping the emotional, marital, economic and social rewards of our lifestyle. If parents do not take responsibility for training and building the lives of their children, others (militants, peers and television) will. Let us not be deceived, spirit forces are behind the world systems moulding our society (Jn 12:31).

God's reps

Jesus expressed our call when he prayed to the Father, 'I do not pray that you should take them out of the world, but that you should keep them from the evil one' (Jn 17:15). We will not conquer our land by withdrawing. The Christian is 'in' the world but not 'of' it. Just as Jesus was sent into the world, so we have been sent (Jn 17:18). We are not called to withdraw be it into a 'mediaeval monastery' or 'charismatic commune'. The church is like a rescue boat. The boat is in the water and it is an effective tool in reaching those who are drowning as long as the water does not enter the boat. When worldliness pervades the church, it risks sinking. We are called to be influencers, not those who are influenced; God's representatives to a lost world. Joseph and Daniel are examples of men in top political positions who were rightly used as influencers from the inside. What a need there is for Christians to be in positions of leadership and influence in our land. What a responsibility we all have to pray for our kings and all in authority (1 Tim 2:1–2). Prayer is still our strongest method of influence. As John Penn put it, 'True godliness does not turn men out of the world, but enables them to live in it, and excites their endeavours to mend it.'

Go

Consider the great sense of responsibility you would feel if you were called to give witness to some crime you had seen committed. The call to be a witness is no trivial matter— people's eternal destinies are at stake. Where is the urgency we see in Jesus' words, 'I must work the works of him who sent me while it is day; the night is coming when no one can work' (Jn 9:4). Do we have the compassion that Jesus had when he cried over Jerusalem: 'How often I wanted to gather your children together, as a hen gathers her brood under her wings, but you were not willing' (Lk 13:34). Have we lost that sense of urgency?

How does it affect us that around 6,500 people will enter eternity in the next hour with many never having heard the gospel once? Paul went as far as saying he was willing to be accursed, that his people might be saved. I say this not to motivate us to evangelize by guilt nor to send us out saying, 'I suppose I'll have to' but to provoke us to seek God for a burden like his for the many lost with whom we daily rub shoulders, who are on their way to hell unless they receive Christ. They include our neighbours, employer or employees, others in our family, those from our streets, schools, the milkman, the dustman. No doubt each one of us has in the past missed opportunities to share the Lord. However, let us not dwell on those failures. There is forgiveness at the cross. Let us now move on with renewed vision to reach others for Christ. Although the Lord is sovereign, he has made us responsible for sharing the gospel. How many are reached in our area for Christ is largely dependent on us. The Lord is not obliged to work through human channels, but he has chosen to do so.

Ask the Lord to give you opportunities to sow seeds that you or others can later reap and don't be discouraged by those who appear not to be responding. It is so easy to give up but many people will only respond after a consistent love has been shown to them over a period of months or even years. Some of those I shared the Lord with years ago, who appeared not to be affected by my words, are now Christians. Who knows what the eventual outcome of our sowing will be? However, as you witness, be sensitive to the Lord and don't be afraid to challenge people to receive Christ (or be surprised when they want to!).

Not everyone to whom we witness will be saved. People have a free will and will reject the gospel if they wish, but you cannot then be held responsible for failing to share it with them. The Lord said, 'When I say to the wicked, "You shall surely die," and you give him no warning; nor speak to warn the wicked from his wicked way, to save his life, that same wicked man shall die in his iniquity; but his blood I will require at your hand. Yet, if you warn the wicked, and he does not turn from his wickedness nor from his wicked way, he shall die in his iniquity, but you have delivered your soul' (Ezek 3:18–19).

For too long fears of being rejected and worries about what people will say have held Christians back from witnessing. Satan is aware that most Christians would rather see relatives and friends go to hell than say anything which might cause them embarrassment. So many Christians are fishing for compliments rather than for men! I am so glad that someone cared enough to share the gospel with me, aren't you? Our call is 'by all means to win some'. I am sure that we haven't exhausted the means yet. However, it will be costly. If we really want to be effective in reaching the lost and in caring for the new converts there will have to be a change in our priorities, use of time, finance, and often a change in church structures and programmes. Do we really believe that one soul is worth more than the whole world?

Pray therefore

After making his disciples aware of the waiting harvest, Jesus charged them to pray. Prayer is practical. It is not a waste of time. Pray for opportunities to share the Lord. I believe if you ask for them, he will give them. You may want to make a list of those you desire to reach so that you can pray for them regularly. Ask the Lord to lay a burden on your heart for those you are especially to pray for. We have authority to bind the powers of darkness that blind people's eyes and prevent them from seeing their need to turn to the Lord. 'For the weapons of our warfare are not carnal but mighty in God for pulling down strongholds, casting down arguments and every high thing that exalts itself against the knowledge of God' (2 Cor 10:4–5). It is the Holy Spirit who enlightens the mind, moving on a man's emotions and making him aware of his need for God. However, we have weapons that can destroy men's arguments and the things that hinder them from seeing their need of salvation. Therefore pray! The Lord challenges us: 'Ask of me, and I will give you the nations for your inheritance' (Ps 2:8).

We need to see that evangelism is not a game of mental chess—countering and outmanoeuvring your opponent's arguments to get him into checkmate. That approach rarely works, as Christianity is not a philosophy or set of beliefs, but primarily a Father/child relationship with God. Words are of little value without the Holy Spirit working in a person's heart to make him aware of his need of the Lord. Only God can convict and convert sinners. However, we are the vessels he works through. Prayer is not a substitute for reaching out, rather the two are vital and should go hand in hand. There is much truth in the old statement, 'Plead with God for souls, before you plead with souls for God.' S. D. Gordon put it this way: 'Prayer is striking the winning blow…service is gathering up the results.'

There is no alternative to prayer. A survey over a period of fifteen years among the largest churches in the world to find out common keys to growth, concluded that although many had similar methods, the one common denominator, was that the churches met in small groups to pray for the unsaved by name. It is not enough to pray in generalities. We need to be specific, to seek God for his burdens, so that we can co-operate in prayer with him. Pray for God to raise up evangelists with a ministry of reaping, to go out into the ripened harvest. John Wesley once said, 'Give me one hundred preachers who fear nothing but sin and desire nothing but God, and I care not a straw whether they be clergymen or laymen; such men will shake the gates of hell and set up the kingdom of heaven on earth.'

Let us catch a new vision to pray for our leaders and to pray for those the Lord is raising up in our land. I echo the apostle Paul's words: 'Brethren pray for us.' Without prayer and God's anointing nothing eternal will be accomplished. Leaders, let us commit ourselves to be those who 'fear sin' and unreservedly desire 'nothing but God' and his will to be done, however costly that may be to our own desires, ambitions and reputation.

God is calling for the members of his church to 'sign up' unreservedly, recognize their commission to be missionaries (wherever that call might take them) and seize the opportunities the Lord gives to share the gospel. We need to say afresh, 'Here am I! Send me' (Is 6:8). As a church we should pray, 'Send us.' Let us ask the Lord to equip and unite us, to raise up a mighty army in our area and to see the territory taken for Christ.

One day every knee shall bow and every tongue confess that Jesus Christ is Lord. Until that day, until he comes, we have a commission to be missionaries for him.

15

Reveille

Are you aware of what God is doing today? Within the church there is much activity and yet in reality so much of it is futile, unproductive and ineffective. Many Christians in their local churches are like men who have fallen overboard at sea unnoticed. Left stranded, in the midst of a vast ocean, they are anxious not to drown, but don't know which way to swim. Treading water, they hope that something will happen before it is too late. For many their only vision is that Jesus will come and get them out of the mess before they drown completely.

The church of God has been called by God to do more than just wait for a quick escape before everything collapses at its feet! We have a job to do.

Awake!

I remember once during a train journey falling asleep and not waking up until I had passed my destination. Many today are spiritually asleep, going through the motions, but continuing along the tracks of tradition, legalism, complacency or apathy. To continue like this will be to miss God.

Are we involved in what God is doing or in what God once did? I believe the church of God is on the verge of something big! The soldier who continues to ignore the reveille call is of little use in an army. This is equally true of sleeping Christians. The church is here for much more than just believing the right doctrines or singing the right songs. For too long the enemy has held territory in our land.

Paul exhorts us to, 'Be sober, be vigilant; because your adversary the devil walks about like a roaring lion, seeking whom he may devour' (1 Pet 5:8). To be sober means to be alert to what is happening, aware of what is going on. It is a military term and refers to being on guard duty. The guard who is not alert is a risk to his king and country. God does not want us to be ignorant or deceived. Satan is out to destroy us, and this land.

It has been said that what is holding us back from real revival in our land is not that the country is unready: the chaos and decay all around is ideal in causing a nation to recognize its need of God. No, it is not the world that is unready for revival, but the church. Therefore, God is equipping, and shaping his saints to be the army he requires in seeing the kingdom taken for God.

Today God's prophetic word is going out to make us aware of what he is doing. The reveille is sounding. It's time to awake and get up. 'Awake, you who sleep, arise from the dead, and Christ will give you light' (Eph 5:14). God wants us to be aware of the battle that is ensuing; aware that Jesus Christ is Lord and of his total victory; aware of what he has called us for and of our delegated authority in Christ. He wants us to realize the power in standing together. I believe that if we really become aware of these truths in God's word our lives will be transformed and we will be equipped for warfare. I believe we are moving into the final chapter of this world's history, it's time to wake up.

Arise

For too long God's people have made little impact and been regarded as an insignificant group. For too long the church has stood back, allowing Satan to take territory. God is

raising up an army to send out amongst those who are lost
and bound, to take the kingdom and set the captives free.
Starting with those 120 believers all out for God in the upper
room, the whole known world of the day was evangelized in a
generation. Our world needs to see the power of God out on
the streets, not just hidden in our church buildings. For too
long the church has been kept inside its buildings and been
told, 'You have nothing relevant to say to our world' while
the 'experts' have told the world how to behave, how to
'demand their rights', how to discipline (or not discipline)
their children. As a result we have the breakdown of our
society, family life, and a lonely depressed and insecure
world.

What does the future hold?

In King Jesus and the message of the gospel of the kingdom
are all answers our world needs for social, political, emotional,
racial, sexual, economic, family and psychological wholeness. Our world is waiting to see a demonstration of the reality
of the kingdom of God. There is another King…Jesus. Let us
not hide our light, but let it shine. Let us be that city set on a
hill, which cannot be hid. Let us rise up, realizing that the
Spirit of the Lord is upon us 'to preach the Gospel to the
poor'. He has sent us to 'heal the brokenhearted, to preach
deliverance to the captives and recovery of sight to the blind,
to set at liberty those who are oppressed, to preach the
acceptable year of the Lord' (Lk 4:18–19). It is God's desire
that this scripture be fulfilled in our midst, in our streets and
towns and cities.

Throughout the world we are seeing revival as never before.
In Latin America the evangelical church is expanding three
times faster than the birth rate, likewise in Kenya and other
parts of Africa and South East Asia.

But this is costly. It may call for a sacrificing of our way of
doing things or our traditions, whether they be hundreds of
years old or hours! It calls for a waking from our apathy, a
submitting to the King and a uniting to be his army. Up until
this point, the outward evidence of the success of our warfare

in this land has seemed small. However, let us take heart, our warring has not been in vain. The tide has turned in our land. It was exciting as I travelled round the country during the latter part of 1981, to see how, every time I said, 'The tide has turned' people came up to me afterwards saying, 'The Lord said that to us as a church through prophecy this week.' It seemed that through the country God was speaking and encouraging his saints that the tide has turned.

Although the observer cannot instantly see much evidence of the tide's turning as he stands watching the sea, after a short while, the fact that it is now coming in becomes quite plain. Reports are common of people stranded because they were not aware the tide was coming in until it was too late. Therefore, saints, let us not sit back in apathy, bemoaning the 'good old days', remembering the times when God has moved in the past, or dwelling on past failures. Let us realize that right now we are evidencing a move of God greater than anything this world has ever seen before.

Eileen Vincent in her book, *God can do it here* (published by Marshall, Morgan & Scott) quotes a vision that a school teacher recently had of a man in a small square room hanging wallpaper to cover up the cracks in the walls. 'It was a thankless task as fresh cracks were appearing all the time, where the walls were beginning to fall away. The man ran from one crack to another in a makeshift cover up job.' As the school teacher watched, God said, 'The devil is busy running around papering over the cracks of his tottering kingdom, he doesn't want you to know the chaos your onslaught in prayer is causing.' As he looked further he noticed that there was only one roll of paper left on the table. The devil was running out of wallpaper!

Therefore, let us with renewed vision join together and rise up a mighty army to charge in and take territory until Christ returns and the triumphant cry goes forth, 'The kingdom of the world has become the kingdom of our Lord and of his Christ and he will reign for ever and ever' (Rev 11:15 NIV).

Soldiers of Christ arise,
   And put your armour on,
Strong in the strength which God supplies
   Through His eternal Son

Strong in the Lord of Hosts,
   And in His mighty power;
Who in the strength of Jesus trusts
   Is more than conqueror.

Stand then in His great might,
   With all His strength endued;
And take to arm you for the fight
   The panoply of God.

———

To keep your armour bright,
   Attend with constant care,
Still walking in your Captain's sight,
   And watching unto prayer.

From strength to strength go on;
   Wrestle, and fight, and pray;
Tread all the pow'rs of darkness down
   And win the well-fought day;

That having all things done,
   And all your conflicts past,
Ye may o'ercome through Christ alone,
   And stand entire at last.

C. Wesley